JAM TOMORROW?

JAM TOMORROW?

JAM TOMORROW?

WHY TIME REALLY MATTERS
IN ECONOMICS

CHARLES CROWSON

First published in Great Britain in 2023 by
Charles Crowson, in partnership with whitefox publishing

www.wearewhitefox.com

Copyright © Charles Crowson, 2023

ISBN 978-1-915635-62-4
Also available as an eBook
ISBN 978-1-915635-63-1

Cover design and typesetting by Couper Street Type Co.
Project management by whitefox
Printed and bound by CPI Group (UK) Ltd, Croydon CR0 4YY

Whatever has value in our world now does not have value in itself, according to its nature – nature is always value-less, but has been given value at some time, as a present, and it is we who gave it and bestowed it.

FRIEDRICH NIETZSCHE

CONTENTS

INTRODUCTION:

THE MARSHMALLOW TEST REDUX

In the late 1960s, Stanford psychologist Walter Mischel conducted a series of tests on young children using marshmallows. The aim was to see if there was a link between the child's ability to delay gratification and their subsequent academic achievement. Each child was given a marshmallow and told that if they did not eat it right away, they would get an extra marshmallow later as a reward. The researcher would then leave the child alone in the room for around fifteen minutes. Those children who had not eaten the first marshmallow were then rewarded with an additional one. Footage of youngsters shifting in their seats, rolling their eyes, sometimes smelling or licking the marshmallow as they battled with temptation was only surpassed visually by the moment when the camera showed one of them cracking and giving in, the torture of waiting proving to be just too much. This was not quite Orwell's Room 101 but, given this was a test done on five-year-olds, the emotional battle was there to be seen.

The second part of Mischel's research was to follow up with the same children when they were teenagers, to see if there was a link between the initial results (those who scoffed the marshmallow immediately and those who waited for an extra one) and how their intellectual and other cognitive skills had developed in the meantime[1]. The results were striking: those children who had waited for the extra treat tended to perform better academically, had better social skills and were better able to cope with stress than those who had eaten the marshmallow straight away. The results, however, were caveated with the observation that other factors beyond innate self-control (such as the child's home environment) might be a factor in subsequent academic achievement, but these were beyond the scope of the test.

These caveats became more nuanced in later iterations of the marshmallow test. A test done on a larger cohort of children that also factored in the educational background of the children's mothers found a much weaker link between innate self-control and subsequent academic achievement[2]. Another comparison of test results over the decades found that, despite the advent of attention-sapping computer games and the like, children taking the test in the 2000s were on average able to hold out from temptation for an average of two minutes longer than those in the 1960s and one minute longer than those in the 1980s. This perhaps suggests that longer-term factors such as rising IQs, technological change or even rising standards of living could be playing a role[3].

The initial hypothesis of the marshmallow test (a link between self-control and subsequent life achievement) has been questioned by later versions of the test by subtly changing its sample size, scope and parameters. Wider social, economic and behavioural factors have been highlighted and

incorporated into the analysis meaning the results and con-
clusions have become far more nuanced. With our knowledge
improved as a result of both the hypothesis and experiment
being fine-tuned over time, this is science at its best; yet much
of the knowledge gained relies heavily upon the brilliant
simplicity of the test itself.

While the marshmallow test was designed to investigate
the relationship between the psychology of delayed gratification and individual achievement, the test itself is really an
economic one – a choice between consuming something now
or consuming it later, with an extra marshmallow standing
in for the concept of added interest. All living things need
to consume to survive, but it is only humans that are aware
of the possibility of better outcomes in the future occurring
from their decisions in the present. This innate awareness
of the potential value of time can be shown by the sort of
choice presented in the marshmallow test intuitively making
sense even to a five-year-old. Squirrels store nuts and dogs
bury bones, but this is a matter of evolutionary habit, and
clearly this process does not involve the idea of the number
of nuts or bones growing over time as a reward for delayed
gratification in the way that compound interest serves to
reward us for saving. It is only humans who *choose to save* for
the future. That these choices are affected by the immediate
environment or personal experience only makes the findings
of the various iterations of the marshmallow test more relevant. Saving is the decision to delay gratification, and this
is ultimately a choice about time. The central idea in this
book is that these decisions about consumption and saving

– jam today or jam tomorrow – lie at the very heart of the economic process[4].

Besides showing how economic decisions are ultimately ones about saving and thus about time, the fact that the marshmallow test revolves around the mundane event of eating something also obliquely reflects the importance of energy transfer in the economic process. Energy transfer, of the sort that happens when we absorb calories by eating a marshmallow, is a necessity for life but also constitutes the rationale underpinning the purpose of the economy, that of ongoing subsistence. If one believes that the economy should serve society, then the immediate material wellbeing of the people stands at the top of the list of things that a successfully functioning economy should provide. Once we move beyond the immediate needs of subsistence, we can start to think meaningfully about saving for the future. Generally speaking, if we cannot subsist, we can borrow to do so – providing there is someone willing to lend to us – but, because this borrowing demands repayment with interest later on, it reduces our ability to consume in the future.

More generally, though, a focus on energy transfer and particularly its *sustainability over time* casts economics and the human decisions that underpin it in a different light. Much in the way Galileo shifted man from the centre to the relative periphery of the solar system by replacing the geocentric model with a heliocentric one, so our growing awareness of the vulnerable state of the natural environment and the finite quantity of the earth's resources puts into perspective man's pursuit of economic growth, which itself is essentially a matter of ever-increasing consumption facilitated for much of the past three centuries by the energy transfer resulting from the burning of fossil fuels.

While economics as a discipline is becoming increasingly mindful of the negative effect of economic activity on the natural environment, much still needs to be done in terms of understanding how our financial system, particularly the use of debt (as a tool of 'borrowing' consumption from the future and bringing it into the present), affects the scale and breadth of human economic activity and how this needs to be managed in an era of resource scarcity and environmental degradation. It seems particularly apposite that the question of whether we are living on borrowed time is coming increasingly to the fore.

Why the focus on time? Much of what we now know about time appears to be totally at odds with how we 'experience' it on a day-to-day level. The work of Einstein and subsequent advances in our understanding of how the universe functions at a quantum level teaches us that there isn't one time, that time doesn't necessarily have a direction, *flowing* from past to future via a sort of common, 'rolling' present[5]. Thanks to Einstein, we now know that time does not pass uniformly in all places, and therefore that it is not the same in different places when measured there. Yet our everyday experience of time is such that all these things appear not to be the case.

The radical departure in this book is to suggest that this difference between how time really functions and how we as humans perceive it can not only be reconciled by a better understanding of the role time plays within the economic sphere, but that the way we actually perceive and experience time has its origin in the very nature of human self-awareness and our choices about consumption and subsistence, and these choices are in turn grounded in the immutable laws of physics.

While the basic choice between consuming in the present or saving for the future makes economic decisions essentially ones about time, this often only becomes apparent in periods of crisis or upheaval, when it feels as though the heavens are falling in. Chapter 1 explores how the climate crisis the world currently faces is a stark reminder of this fact, with global warming creating a sort of end-of-days scenario reminiscent of millenarian Christian thinking in medieval Europe. Our perception of time varies as the needs of the present balance with our hopes for the future, and the time horizon reflecting this not only constantly changes but also forms a continuous thread running through economic history. While for most of the past three hundred years since the industrial revolution our economic horizons have been expanding, events such as the global financial crisis in 2007–9 show how quickly the good times can end. While that crisis was solved through massive bailouts, if left unchecked, such situations can develop into a complete societal and economic collapse as the banking system implodes and money ceases to function. From an economic and monetary point of view, that final destination was faced by Germany in 1945 following its loss of the Second World War.

Analysing the way in which we balance our proclivity to consume goods and services on the one hand or to invest in our futures through saving on the other is key to understanding how our perception of time underpins our economic decisions. This requires balancing what can be considered at a general level with what is idiosyncratic to a particular economy at a given time. Chapter 2 provides a paradigm of how this can be done, using the UK housing market as an example, with a particular focus on how housing has essentially shifted from being a good to be consumed (albeit over time) to something more like an investment for the future. The vector of this change in how we value houses has been the growth of debt since the 1970s, and the chapter goes on to show how an economic worldview based on time allows money and credit to be fully integrated into a new theory of value.

While much of current economic theory starts with price and works backwards to explain our choices with respect to the rational allocation of scarce resources, a theory of value based on time focuses instead on the language we employ when describing our economic choices. Rather than using mathematical formulae to explain general economic relationships, Chapter 3 employs the techniques of analytical philosophy, the close examination of ordinary language, to explore how we think about and express value in an economic sense and, in so doing, how they reveal the proper relationship between value and price. This approach shows valuation to be something more like an ethical choice that spurs us into economic activity, and it is this activity in the market that leads to price formation, as bargains are struck and transactions occur.

In the same way that philosophy no longer considers language to be a neutral medium for expressing ideas, money and credit have to be considered as integral and active elements of economic theory. Rather than seeking to define what money is, Chapter 4 looks at the jobs we ask money to do and shows how inflation and deflation reflect how well those jobs are being done. The critical observation is that money itself reflects the temporal nature of our economic decision-making process, and this means that money has *tenses*. As a system of account, money looks to the past and historical prices. As a means of payment and exchange, it sits in the present to facilitate consumption and the discharging of obligations. As a store of wealth, it looks forward to the future. Money is essentially unstable, since the temporal roles it plays pull in opposite directions and inflationary and deflationary pressures are the product of the competing claims put upon money by the demands of the present and the future. Yet it is in successfully balancing these instabilities that money fulfils its function in the economy, and when it fails at one of its key jobs, it eventually tends to fail at all of them.

Chapter 5 explores the nature of saving and how movements in the financial markets reflect our ever-changing economic time horizon. Key to understanding this is the role of market volatility and liquidity as expressions of our competing views on valuation. Healthy markets are ones with low price volatility relative to trading volumes in which investors have strong but opposing views on value. Rapid shifts in price levels relative to trading volume reflect markets where convictions about valuation are low or lopsided. As markets have become more sophisticated, computing power has provided us with the technology to examine historical price data in minute detail, but the question of whether this really allows us to forecast future economic trends or market movements with any certainty is examined in the context of the discipline of history, which apart from certain determinist schools of thought, is far less sanguine about how much the past can tell us about the likely shape of future events.

With the increasing sophistication of its use of data analysis and statistical methods, economics often seems to be a discipline aspiring to be a peer of the hard sciences. Chapter 6 questions whether this is a viable proposition, especially from the perspective of testability and the metrics by which economic theories are validated. A scientific basis for economics can, however, be established: that the basic goal of a successful economy is the subsistence of the society it serves, allowing economic thinking to be grounded in the law of the conservation of energy. Understanding the economic implications of entropy also provides a key pillar to underpin a theory of value based on time, since the concept of entropy itself not only provides a way of understanding consumption in an economy but also arguably provides a means of understanding why time itself often appears to have a direction, hence our basic economic choice between consuming and saving. Einstein's theory of relativity in turn provides a much clearer way of explaining the interactions between the various agents in the economy in terms of their relative perception of time.

If we were to have a free and limitless source of energy that guaranteed human subsistence and consumption in perpetuity, there would likely be much less impetus to save for the future and thus time would no longer be as central a factor in our economic calculus. While progress is being made in terms of energy efficiency and sustainability, the immediate issues of climate change and resource scarcity the world is facing means we are not only having to ask who gets what part of the economic pie but increasingly how big that pie should be. Chapter 7 looks at this question through the lens of the money system, debt and consumption, and seeks to draw a parallel between the narrative of how the gold standard failed and how the current fiat-money system may struggle to sustain a socio-economic system based on mass democracy and mass consumption. Money does the jobs we ask it to do, and if it fails, it is replaced by a new money system better suited to the needs of society. This is perhaps a situation which we are now confronting at the start of the twenty-first century.

★   ★   ★

The overall goal is to put forward a new relative theory of value based on our perception of time. If saving is the definitive economic act, then our sense of value represents a shifting time horizon or balance between the demands and desires of the present on the one hand and the possibilities of the future on the other. When economic choices boil down to decisions between consuming and saving, then the various cycles within the economy effectively trace the constantly changing time horizons of its economic agents, from individuals and households to corporations and governments. Periods of growth see the collective time horizon extending:

businesses invest more and hire more employees; consumers spend more; the stock market climbs the 'wall of worry'. Recessions and crises see them contracting: lenders raise credit standards and call-in debts; companies retrench their balance sheets and lay-off workers; households start to pay off their credit-card debt and generally 'rein in their horns'. Debt as *borrowed time* and interest as an associated *cost of time* are merely a reflection of this more fundamental yet elusive truth about our constantly changing economic perception of time.

But within these broad collective shifts in outlook between consumption and saving, the scale, pace and magnitude of change differs for each type of economic agent. Crucially, however, it is not simply the time horizons of these individual agents that matter; it is the different needs and desires of these assorted economic players *relative to one another* and how this dictates the horizons and choices of those with whom they interact. In the same way that Einstein's theories of relativity made time 'proper' to the bodies concerned rather than 'real' in an absolute, Newtonian sense, so this approach makes economics into a study, not of modelling static systems, but of the ever-varying relationships between economic agents as they pass through time.

I.

TIMELY MEDITATIONS

'If you can't explain something to a six-year-old, then you don't understand it yourself.' Even if Einstein never actually said this, it is nonetheless a useful maxim. Such failures may be due to the manner of the explanation, an inability to engage with the complexity of the subject or a combination of the two. The onset of the global financial crisis in 2007–9, which at one stage threatened a collapse of the entire global financial system, might be considered not only a failure to explain, but also a failure to understand, to warn or perhaps even to prevent. The general feeling at the time was summed up by Queen Elizabeth II when she asked pointedly, 'Why did nobody notice it?'[1]

Before the crisis, there were of course some harbingers of doom, as inevitably there must be. But in terms of responsibility, it is perhaps those most closely linked to public policy and regulation who ought to be in the spotlight, even if the blame game itself focused on the greed and speculation in the banking sector. But what of economics and the theories which dominate the discipline? Clearly economic theory influences policy, even if it doesn't always form the basis of it. Economic failures of this magnitude ought to provoke not only soul-searching by economists but also a fundamental reappraisal of the ideas underpinning the discipline of economics itself.

Modern economics is highly specialised, with its many niches mirroring the great complexity of the modern global economy. If such a degree of specialisation causes problems of comprehension within the economics profession itself, then it is clearly going to make it seem remote to the layman, particularly given the highly mathematical and statistical nature of the work involved. Yet, much like the challenge of explaining something to a six-year-old, this need not be the case.

In *The Last Stone*, Mark Bowden's account of the extraordinary interrogation of Lloyd Welch in the Sheila and Kate Lyon murder case in the US, the author sets the scene for events leading up to the killings by explaining to the modern reader (and perhaps reminding the older reader) what the vibe was like in the early 1970s when the murders took place:

> *Ground was shifting under enduring institutions of*
> *American life, and the promise that had propelled the country*
> *so dynamically through the 1950s and 1960s had soured. Jobs*
> *were scarce, and paychecks didn't go so far – a phenomenon*
> *dubbed 'stagflation'. Americans had stopped buying stocks –*
> *they were no longer betting on the future.*[2]

While this description of life in the 1970s is incidental to the book's main narrative, it is nonetheless immediately accessible to any reader. The sense of malaise and decline is palpable, even poetic. If one were to ask what the 1970s were like economically in the US, Bowden's description is virtually complete. If three short sentences can evoke almost perfectly the economic backdrop of a whole decade, why does economics have such a problem doing so with all its equations?

When economics does provide an explanation, we often end up with a series of parallel scenarios argued over by rival cliques within the discipline due to the tendency to believe that events must fit into particular models of economic behaviour, regardless of the example in question. Economics can explain the problems of the 1970s in the US as being variously caused by the end of the Bretton Woods currency agreement in 1971 (known as the Nixon shock), the oil shocks (of 1973–4 and later in the decade), excessive deficit financing by President Johnson ('guns and butter'), by policies set in motion even earlier in the 1960s by President Kennedy, by demographic changes (a surge in demand as the baby boomer generation came of age), by a huge expansion of private-sector lending or by onerous costs relating to environmental remediation policies initiated during the decade. For a historian, this is a set of reasons to be balanced, while for an economist, be they a neo-Keynsian, a monetarist, a neo-classicist or of some other school, there is a sense that the facts need to fit a model valid not only in the past but, critically, also in the future.

This issue goes to the heart of what economics is. In part, this is a question of whether economics is a science, a branch of the humanities or something in between. On a more fundamental level, it raises a question about the nature of the problem economics is trying to address and whether the questions it tends to ask, and the means by which it tries to answer them, are the right ones for this purpose.

Through a statistical analysis of prices, economics is generally very good at ascertaining the *facts*. With its tendency to create systems and mathematical formulae to represent them, it spends much time focusing on the *means* by which the economy functions. Where it falls down, and where by contrast the Bowden quotation above rings so true, is in understanding the *ends* to which economic activity is directed. This last question is the *why* of economics – why do economic agents act in the way they do? By answering the why question better, the true meaning of the empirical facts of economics (i.e., prices) becomes clearer. Answering the why question also helps us to understand better the *how* question: the means by which the economy and economic interactions actually function[3].

At the core of the argument are two ideas: the importance of value or value judgements on the one hand, and the importance of time on the other. Value and time are not just linked economically; they are inseparable, to the extent to which all judgements about economic value are ultimately decisions about time. Aware of their ability to satisfy their own future needs and desires, humans have to choose between consuming in the present or delaying that consumption to the future. These decisions are in a large part based upon our own experience, but also on our knowledge of the past. As saving is the act of delaying consumption to the future, it is therefore saving that defines the scope of the economic sphere. The act of saving also defines all value judgements within this economic sphere and the way we make decisions about saving lies at the heart of the *why* of economics.

What makes Mark Bowden's brief description of life in the 1970s leap off the page is that it is a true statement about value and time. The economic shock of inflation in that decade meant that households struggled to put food on the table and gas in their cars, and stubbornly high unemployment added to the problem. The 'American Dream', aspirations of a better future and the pursuit of happiness, was clearly on hold. Things were so bad that 'Americans had stopped buying stocks. *They were no longer betting on the future* [emphasis added].' This feeling of angst clearly comes from being forced to scrabble around in the present with little hope of better times coming around the corner. No wonder Americans felt their institutions and value-systems were under threat.

Economics is often described as an exercise in the allocation of scarce resources. If this is the case, how does it value time, which isn't so much scarce as vanishing? The premise is simple. As far as we can know, only humankind has an awareness of time, in the sense of a perception of past and future from a location in the present. This is what underpins all our economic decisions and interactions. The technical language of economics and finance is of course littered with time-related measurements: the time value of money, the duration of bonds, yield to maturity and so on, but these calculations generally take the form of measurements *in terms of time,* such as stock returns over a given period or bond yields to a certain maturity date. What happens less often is thinking of time as the thing itself to be measured. While in day-to-day conversation we often speak in these sort of terms – for example when we say we are making up for lost time or that someone is living on borrowed time – such thinking is rarely expressed directly in economics.

Time is clearly different; it isn't a commodity to be traded or something in which one can invest directly, at least not in any conventional sense. Nor can valuing time spent or time left be reduced to a simple calculation through counting on a clock-face. Time has a value all of its own, and this value seems to come from its fleeting nature, the very passing of which draws our attention. John Maynard Keynes was right in saying that in the long run we are all dead[4]. While we are alive however, time matters, and clarifying why that is so is the task at hand.

Why perform this exercise *now*? Broadly speaking, from the ancient world until the industrial revolution, living standards barely rose, or did so at a glacially slow pace. The industrial revolution, which saw the harnessing of energy from fossil fuels using steam power, along with a slew of scientific discoveries and a more general trend towards technological progress, created a self-reinforcing revolution in productivity growth and, with it, a general rise in the standard of living if measured in terms of gross domestic production (GDP) per capita or something similar. Since the industrial revolution, humanity has flourished. We can judge this not only in terms of the overall global population, but in terms of wellbeing – average longevity, standards of health and nutrition, levels of education and so forth. Yet increasingly we are becoming aware of the price that has to be paid for human progress. The Anthropocene Era, the one in which man's influence on the planet is becoming increasingly significant, is now often described as roughly starting in the 1950s[5]. The twenty-first century is one where climate science is increasingly suggesting that human progress, itself often a by-word for *economic* progress or at least measured as such, is coming at the expense of the natural environment and the climatic stability of the planet itself.

What is of interest to the understanding of time in economics is not the veracity of the scientific evidence in favour of man's influence on the global climate, nor the wisdom of the suggested responses in terms of the energy transition away from fossil fuels. What is significant is the sense that man-made climate change, as an unwanted by-product of economic growth over the centuries, is an existential threat to humanity itself. The more secular age that was ushered in by the Enlightenment and industrialisation had at its heart a sense of human progress and development in which mankind has been able to benefit materially from scientific discovery and technological advances. This era of progress stood in contrast, in Western Europe at least, to the more millenarian, religious age that preceded it, one in which the apocalypse depicted in the *Revelation of St John* in the New Testament was not just believed to be a real possibility but one that seemed imminent for much of the time[6].

As the environmental consequences of man's economic progress have become clearer, so too has a sense that, should our quest for economic growth proceed unabated or at the very least continue without more concern for environmental conservation, then the sort of end-of-days scenarios once only prophesised in the scriptures run the risk of becoming reality. If the environmental movement has one central message it is that, if we carry on like this, there may well be a point when time is up – for us and possibly for the planet.

It is an argument based on the assumption of a time horizon that weighs up our current needs and those implicit in our future. Its calculus is dictated by the level of human consumption of natural resources, especially fossil fuels. It may have taken us the best part of three centuries to realise it fully, but economics is not just about scarce resources but finite ones, the most finite of which is the planet we inhabit and whose natural riches we extract and consume, a process that appears increasingly to be detrimental to our own survival as a society and possibly even as a species. It is perhaps only now, with this risk in mind, that time seems in a sense to be *running out*. The aim in this book, though, is to show that time has *always been* the key consideration in economic decision making and that it is the case from the micro level (individuals, households and companies) up to the macro level (governments, nations and geopolitically).

The financial valuation of companies often incorporates an idea of *terminal value* which involves a final estimate of value in a particular number of years' time. The apparently apocalyptic threat to the world's climate has brought a similar sense of finality into economics in terms of man's use of the planet's resources. If one is focusing on the task of valuing time in economics, it is perhaps this idea of time horizon as *something that itself varies* that is the key point of departure. One can start to look at the various economic cycles (the business cycle, the credit cycle, the banking cycle or even the long cycle of monetary systems themselves) in terms of a series of time horizons that extend during periods of economic expansion, as people's optimism and confidence about the future increases, or reduce during contractions, as fears for the economy rise and households and businesses consolidate through the process of paying down debt (otherwise known as balance-sheet repair, a phenomenon usually characterising a recession).

The various participants in the economy, individuals, households, companies, governments and so on, all possess their own separate time horizons, with those of individuals generally being the shortest while those of governments (as in the *system* of government rather than incumbents in office) being the longest. These myriad time horizons not only overlap and therefore influence one another, but vary at different times and for different reasons.

If the climate change threat is anything to go by, then it is perhaps in crises that the importance of time and these shifting time horizons becomes most apparent. During the long period of economic growth and rising prosperity beginning with the industrial revolution, confidence in progress from technology and science has, in a way, reflected ever-extending optimism for mankind's prosperity and general wellbeing. While not ignoring the possibilities of future technological progress, the recent focus on the environmental threat to mankind from climate change is in turn symbolic of that optimism diminishing and, because of its seemingly existential nature, it is obviously far more worrying.

In economic terms, it is perhaps the case that the rapid contraction of our perceived time horizon (during a recession or a market crash) highlights the importance of time itself as a factor in our economic rationale in a way that steady economic expansion (symbolic of a gradual extension in our time horizon) simply does not. While there does seem to be some asymmetry in this view (economic or market crashes happen faster than expansions), it may in fact be a question of extremes at both ends. It is perhaps at the soaring heights of a boom or in the depths of a recession when we are most aware of our changing economic future in a way which we are not during the more temperate periods of mediocre growth or slight downturn.

One could, for example, look at the credit crunch that marked the start of the global financial crisis of 2007–9 as the very paradigm of a situation in which our collective economic time horizon collapsed from a rosy one based on the assumption that tomorrow would be like today forever into a desperate day-to-day struggle to liquidate assets to pay down debts as creditors started to call in their loans. For the Northern Rock bank in the UK, that time horizon in fact fell to zero; for the first time in over a century, a British financial institution suffered a bank run, which ended in insolvency and subsequent nationalisation. In that situation, when a highly leveraged institution such as a commercial bank cannot find lenders, even on an overnight basis – hence insolvency, then any possibilities for the future cease to exist at all.

In a somewhat dark chapter in my personal financial history, I had the dubious honour of buying a holiday rental property in the UK in July 2007, financed with what turned out to be one of the very last Northern Rock mortgages to be issued. With the credit crunch, what was supposed to have been a sensible and safe long-term investment offering a bit of yield from rental income almost immediately became an albatross of negative cashflow and negative equity as house prices collapsed. For a while at least, my personal investment time horizon had inadvertently foreshortened to one where my main preoccupation was to manage the balance in my bank account on a month-to-month basis as mortgage payments went out but the expected offsetting rental payments remained stubbornly absent. Yet, in time, and in no small part due to the bank bailouts, the British economy recovered and, with it, the housing market. Gradually, the short-term disaster that had been my foray into the property market turned out to be a reasonable long-run investment.

In what seemed at the time to be an existential event for the world economy, it is hardly a surprise that my personal experiences during the global financial crisis closely mirrored events at large. In September and October 2008, during the period between the collapse of Lehman Brothers bank and the passage of the Troubled Asset Relief Program (TARP) through Congress, there was a feeling that the US banking system might actually collapse, that ATM machines might stop giving out cash and that people's savings would be lost. A few years later during the Eurozone crisis, with the government bond markets of various Euro-area countries in free fall and with the possibility of Greece leaving the Eurozone altogether, there was a similar feeling that the euro currency project itself might be in jeopardy.

In financial markets at least, times of extreme crisis such as these are characterised by outlandish price volatility, as investors try desperately to reduce their exposure to risky assets and move their capital into traditional 'safe havens' such as US government bonds or gold. Investors' collective time horizons tend to foreshorten dramatically during periods of extreme market duress. In terms of the provision of credit and lending in general, the tightening of credit conditions in a market downturn or recession, as characterised by lenders being willing to lend less overall (and, even then, only to less-risky borrowers) is the very definition of a shortening of the general economic time horizon.

Yet, despite the near-terminal crisis in 2008, the US banking system survived. Famously in July 2012, in his 'whatever it takes' speech, then President of the European Central Bank, Mario Draghi, galvanized market confidence in the euro project and averted a possible collapse in the European government bond market, which might in turn have threatened the euro itself[7]. Even though underlying structural economic problems remained and new potential issues emerged, in both of these instances the immediate threat of financial and economic collapse was avoided and recoveries eventually occurred, and with them came the return of confidence. If one is thinking in terms of the importance of time in our collective economic consciousness, near misses such as the Lehman Brothers bankruptcy or the Eurozone crisis can be held in contrast to actual collapses, particularly those whose severity involves the fracturing of the monetary system such that society is forced into a type of hand-to-mouth existence largely dependent on barter.

One such example of total collapse is Germany at the end of the Second World War, when the vaulting ambitions of Hitler's thousand-year Reich lay in tatters in the bombed-out ruins of Berlin. The monetary system effectively collapsed to be replaced by barter and the supply of basic necessities was severely disrupted. Day-to-day subsistence became the priority for most Germans[8]. In the immediate aftermath of the war, economic decision-making revolved around survival-levels of consumption rather than any real notion of saving for the future. That for Germans at the time this episode of history came to be known as 'Stunde Null' (zero hour) tells one all one needs to know about the mentality of that desperate period.

Yet for the Germans of 1945, zero hour also marked a social, economic and political collapse that provided a psychological break with their Nazi past, and in that period of struggle, the foundations of a new, democratic and prosperous Germany (at least in what was to become the Federal Republic of Germany) were being laid, however remote and impossible that future may have seemed at the time. What followed was the 'economic miracle' and three decades of growth during which Germans' economic possibilities improved as never before.

While it might not seem immediately obvious that events in Germany in 1945 and those of the 2007–9 global financial crisis are in any way linked and that, as historical events, the causality was very different, in economic terms, especially if one is putting time and the concept of a time horizon at the centre of one's analysis, the banking crisis of 2007–9 can be seen as an event on a road that might eventually have ended up in a German zero-hour situation, at least in economic and monetary terms. Had there not been a bank bailout in 2008, the United States (and possibly the world) could have ended up in a depression-like situation of widespread banking failure and permanently high unemployment not dissimilar to that which the country experienced following the global banking collapse of 1931. The risk of a hyperinflation might also have emerged, and the sort of chaotic scenes suffered by Zimbabwe in 2008 and Venezuela in the Maduro era might have happened in the US had the banks gone bust and ATM machines actually ended up not being able to dispense cash.

Rather than looking at economic crises as outlying events or exceptions that prove the rule, they can instead be treated as situations where some of the deeper and more fundamental characteristics of the economic process are revealed in a way that is far less apparent in periods of stability or continuity. Absent a crisis, many of what we call the 'certainties' of economic life, such as the idea that stocks are a good investment for the long-term or that house prices only go up, are accepted not because they are inherently true but because people do not find the need to question them on a daily basis, particularly if recent experience supports our faith in them.

A good way to illustrate this observation about the 'in between' state where questions aren't asked is to look at the insidious effect of inflation on the value of money, particularly since it is the compounding process through which inflation erodes the purchasing power of money over time, which is so key to understanding the role of time in economics. The 1990s saw central banks in the developed world move to a policy of inflation targeting, where an arbitrary 2% annual inflation rate was deemed to be the appropriate monetary-policy goal. Compound interest, supposedly described by Einstein as an eighth wonder of the world, is essentially a non-linear process affecting all financial assets that offer a yield. The compounding effect of inflation over time is exactly the same as that of compound interest only rather than increasing the amount of money over time as compound interest does, it reduces the real value of the very medium we use to 'keep the score': money itself.

The mental arithmetic of the effect of compounding over an extended period of time is tricky. An investment of $100 yielding 10% grows to $110 at the end of year one. 10% of $110 is $11, meaning one's investment is actually worth $121 at the end of year two and so on. A useful heuristic or rule-of-thumb to calculate compounding over the long term is the 'rule of 72': if one divides 72 by the yield (in this case 10%), one can calculate that the time needed for the investment to double in value is 7.2 years. An investment yielding 5% would take 14.4 years to double, and so on. An investment yielding 2% would take 36 years to double. But if one looks at inflation, a process which *reduces* the purchasing power of money through the same compounding effect, 2% annual inflation (the central bank target level), as interpreted by the rule of 72, suggests that the value of money goes to zero over a period of 36 years, all else being equal. Yet for the most part, people aren't horrified that the value of their money is being destroyed at this pace because, at a day-to-day level, the change is largely imperceptible. In any case, the economy might be growing in real terms at the same time, which usually means wages rise and so on, masking the absolute effect of inflation. It is only in periods of intense inflation, such as the one experienced in the 1970s (and more recently following the Covid-19 pandemic) when people notice how their grocery bills rise on a week-to-week basis, that inflation becomes 'a thing'. The rest of the time, people either fail to notice smaller price changes or don't balk at them and thus popular awareness about the effect of inflation simply is not as problematic from a social or political perspective.

As a non-linear function (one with an exponential effect over time), compounding can be positive, in terms of GDP growth raising the overall standard of living or in terms of saving for one's pension, or negative, if one is looking at the effect of inflation on the purchasing power of money. Time-based calculations already play a key role in financial analysis and yet, while we tend to plot prices in terms of time on graphs, we also allude to time in terms of price (as, for example, when we say a rising stock market shows a growing confidence in the future prospects of the economy). What this shows is that, while we are comfortable using time as a fixed system of measurement against which we measure price, we often overlook the fact that we also treat time itself as having value. Time can act as a variable that itself is subject to change, albeit in a way that sometimes seems less obvious since it is often bound up in language rather than being illustrated on a graph, where time usually sits on the x-axis. Time is precious;

but somehow this sense of value isn't fully conveyed by the units of seconds, minutes and hours.

★   ★   ★

The role of time as a fixed system of measurement in economics has its origins in the intellectual history of the discipline itself, particularly with respect to the way in which it grew to mirror natural philosophy in the early modern period. Like Newtonian physics, classical economics has time as a fixed measure for comparison. This tacit assumption about time also underpins the various schools of economic thought that have evolved subsequently. The tendency to hypothesise that economies exist in a stable state where relationships tend to revert to a balance over time is again one that might appear to have been subconsciously or inadvertently borrowed from Newton, especially from his first law, which suggests that bodies continue in a state of rest or in a uniform motion in a straight line unless acted upon by a force. Though physics has advanced considerably since Newton, economics has yet to adapt to fundamental developments in our understanding of the universe and our wider knowledge of how bodies interact in it, particularly those put forward by Einstein over a hundred years ago.

If one looks at how our understanding of physics has developed from the Newtonian one, the obvious point of departure is to consider Einstein's theories of relativity. Following Einstein, time was no longer some sort of intergalactic tape measure serving to calculate in a constant way, but something that itself varied, depending on what was being measured and where. The possibility of applying this idea to economics is obvious: time, in an economic sense, can be liberated from its traditional position on the x-axis of graphs and assessed as something with a value of its own and whose value changes as the various cycles in the economy progress.

Time needs to be placed at the heart of economic theory as both a quantitative and a qualitative factor that changes and whose change can be assessed. If instead of a fixed measure allowing comparison of prices over a given period, time is regarded as something that itself changes (as our perception of time itself changes), an awareness of time becomes the key metric by which all economic participants make their decisions. It is the constantly varying time horizons of the assorted agents in the economy and their changing needs and desires that provide not only a basis on which to assess economic activity, but the analysis of which defines the boundaries of the economic sphere. Periods of economic stability and growth in which our collective time horizon extend can be compared and contrasted to ones in which, as with the global financial crisis, they collapse in precipitous fashion.

★　　★　　★

The philosophical shift between Newton and Einstein can in some ways be characterised as the absolute giving way to the relative (Einstein's key theory was, after all, one of relativity). One of the consequences of this for economics is to re-evaluate what we consider to be value in an economic sense. Rather than it being an absolute or intrinsic measure, value ought to be looked at as a relative concept, in the sense that what we value tends to vary over time and by location, but which is ultimately bound by the necessities imposed by our temporal outlook of economics. The things we value not only change over time but also vary between different cultures and societies. During the great fire of London in 1666, for example, the diarist Samuel Pepys buried his prized (and highly valuable) stock of parmesan cheese in his back garden for safe keeping[9]. It is pretty unlikely that a modern-day Londoner, faced with a house fire, would first raid the fridge for their stash of cheese even if they were partial to a sprinkling of parmesan on their Bolognese. Clearly, Pepys' cheese was valued in a totally different way.

Without wanting to infer too much from such a trivial example, the point is that it is not necessarily what we value that should be the focus of economics; this is a matter of taste or fashion going beyond utility, especially if one has satisfied the immediate needs of subsistence. The important consideration is that we value things, and an economic theory of value is intrinsically linked to mankind's overall perception of time. The goal here is one of differentiating between the general and the specific, what is common to the human economic experience and what is not, with a view to finding the limits to the application of economic rules to human behaviour. Economics' credibility and scientific rigour can be enhanced as much by what we decide we can't say as by what we can.

The sort of economic analysis that results from this shift

from the absolute to the relative lends itself simultaneously to the very abstract (the nature of value and the valuation of time) and to the very specific (how value is expressed through price in a particular instance). What it tends to avoid is generalisations in the grey area in between and, in so doing, moves beyond the use of mathematical formulae as a means of expressing such generalisations. While the search for patterns, and therefore the search for rules and the formulae which characterise them, has been the stock-in-trade of econometrics for many decades, a relative approach to economics is one that necessarily focuses on differences as much as similarities[10]. One can discern overall themes relating to the dynamic nature of value, the changing role of credit and money or the interrelationship of supply and demand but these have to be balanced with the idiosyncratic features of each example, be they cultural, political or social.

This has two consequences: first, one ends up with a far greater integration of economic history into economic theory than is currently the case; secondly, by acknowledging this central role of history in economics, one is more likely to conclude that events in the past, however recursive they may seem at one level, do not offer a perfect blueprint of what will happen in the future. History's circumspect attitude to predicting the future stands in stark contrast to the rule-making tendencies of economics, where price events in the past are used to create general mathematical formulae whose purpose is in part to anticipate what is to come. Positioning economics somewhere between the hard sciences and the social sciences (particularly history) would likely lead to a more honest appraisal of what economics itself can achieve and also of where its limits lie.

As an illustration of this approach, the next chapter examines the specific example of the UK housing market from around 1970 to the present day. While housing (and shelter more generally) is a universal, taking a particular example such as the UK allows us to examine the idiosyncrasies of how it developed from a historical perspective, particularly with respect to how the legislative process in Britain caused it to develop in the way that it did. One can then contrast the UK market to other housing markets, such as those in the US or Japan, to show how value, while common to all economic experience, finds itself expressed in particular ways both in time and place. Once the differences have been established, that which is held in common can be illustrated more clearly, particularly with respect to how money and credit have affected the overall trends in how we value property and how this has ultimately been expressed in terms of price over the decades.

What makes housing such a good starting point is the underlying question of whether it is a good (to be consumed, albeit over a long period of time) or an investment (for the future) or something in between. If it is has changed from the former to the latter over time, what has made it change and why? The consumption of goods is very much something done in the present, while investing is something, albeit done in the present, that is undertaken with a view to the future. If housing can be considered part good and part investment and therefore both of the present and of the future, it offers a useful point of departure for the question of how time and our perception of it can be used to underpin a new theory of value. It also provides a context in which to begin an analysis of money and credit, both of which have a reflexive relationship to time and our perception of it within the economic sphere.

2.

AN ENGLISHMAN'S HOUSE IS HIS LADDER

The meaning of the saying 'an Englishman's house is his castle' has shifted over time. Originally, the 'castle' alluded to the security provided by English liberty – that authorities were not allowed to enter one's home without a warrant, and this was symbolic of the common-law rights of the individual that arguably made Englishness what it was. More recently, and following the spectacular rise in house prices over the past five or so decades, the sense of 'castle' would now seem to be more meaningful in the context of the monetary value in property (castles are, after all, valuable) rather than an older and more abstract concern about habeas corpus and the like.

The change in meaning reflects a shift in how we value housing, and the idea to be explored in this chapter is how our sense of value, the question of how much something is worth to us, changes over time. The choice of housing (and the UK housing market in particular) to illustrate the dynamic nature of value is due to one specific characteristic. Much of the housing stock in the UK is well over a century old and, while many of the actual piles of bricks and mortar that constitute the physical presence of the housing market are the same, their value (as reflected in their price) has risen dramatically, often far in excess of inflation and out of proportion to the rise in population.

Explaining the dramatic change in value of the same physical object over time, and for reasons other than just currency debasement or supply and demand factors, provides a window into the nature of value and how the various social, economic, technological and legislative processes combine with respect to the dynamic and non-linear process of the reattribution of value. The analysis of changes in the UK housing market over a fifty-odd-year period therefore provides a paradigm for how economic analysis involving the concept of time should be conducted. From a detailed historical analysis of a specific example, one can legitimately make general observations about value and time, but comparisons between examples then shows that *what* we value and *to what extent* we value them varies dramatically, and this in turn helps to illustrate the limitations economics has with respect to its claims to generality, especially when it comes to predicting the path of events in the future.

★　　★　　★

Dramatic changes in how we value things can have the most mundane origins. In an admittedly subjective example, I moved house early in 2018 and had the misfortune of spending the first month or so without any heating or hot water during a freezing weather episode dubbed 'the beast from the east' by the media (a dramatic event by UK standards, others may disagree)[1]. Surrounded by boxes and irate at a succession of engineers unable to fix the boiler, I was understandably not very enamoured with the place, nor keen to 'settle in'. What was funny, though, was that only a few hours after the boiler had finally been fixed and with the rooms warming up nicely, I found myself busily unpacking, deciding what was going where, thinking about what improvements were needed, reflecting what a nice, quiet cobbled London mews it was and so on. If for me the shift from loathing to liking was just a matter of switching the heating on, what did people think about houses before central heating when all they had to rely upon was a fireplace and a few one-bar heaters? What about the US before air-conditioning relieved the horror of those hot, humid summers?

Technological innovations (the Roman hypocaust notwithstanding) that became widespread in the twentieth century meant that houses could be far more comfortable places in which to spend time. The combination of central heating and air-conditioning meant this could be true all year round. This created the possibility for us to treat property as more valuable simply because it was more pleasant to spend time indoors. Value in this respect is clearly more than a purely monetary phenomenon. The growing popularity of home improvement and DIY as a pastime in the UK mirrored this change in the way we started treating our houses. The DIY fad perhaps reflected a culmination of technological advances (in plumbing, sewerage, the provision of gas and electricity, building materials, labour-saving appliances and so on) as well as a general rise in the standard of living (reflected in discretionary spending and leisure time) and social changes (the idea of consumption as an individual expression of taste). Because of this combination of factors, housing *could* be valued more, and together they perhaps describe necessary but not sufficient grounds on which a long-term rise in house prices could happen.

To explain all the rise in house prices since the 1970s as the product of the advent of central heating would of course be absurd, but it is such technological change that provides the circumstances in which a major reattribution of value in price terms might occur[2]. For a full explanation of the great rise in property prices (over and above inflation) since the 1970s, we need to look elsewhere.

From about a quarter of homes being owner-occupied after the First World War, the number of owners finally overtook the number renters in the 1970s, and peaked around the start of the global financial crisis in 2007 at just over 70% before drifting lower in the subsequent decade[3]. Houses are certainly worth more these days. This statement is not an empty truism – it is a statement about value, not price, and acknowledges that price alone is not a full reflection of all that we value. Since the 1970s, there has been an extraordinary shift from housing being, except for the very rich, something where utility was central to something that has become the vector of wealth creation, retirement saving and even social mobility (or the lack of it).

To say something new has happened does not disregard the long story of domesticity amongst England's middling sorts;

the Pooterish tendencies of the English and their houses have a long and varied history[4]. Clearly, being house proud is a way of expressing one's social status or personal self-worth, and that is a reflection of a continuity, not a change. What needs to be examined more closely is how legislative and regulatory changes over recent decades have allowed this instinct towards homemaking and property ownership to transform housing into the key asset class in the UK economy and, in particular, how this has led to house prices rising as far as they have.

In the UK at least, the goal of 'getting on the property ladder' is now almost so pervasive as to have become socially normative. Indeed, the very word 'property' outside its technical legal usage is now synonymous with housing-as-investment and the market for it. This reflects a critical observation that the attribution of value is essentially a collective, social act with normative tendencies, even if ownership is itself an individual act. With property and house prices the standard fodder of dinner-party conversation across the land, it is important to see the attribution of value as a process in language, even though value is often expressed in monetary terms. The logic behind the ladder is quite simple: house prices just go up, and whenever they've fallen, the subsequent housing market rally has generally been strong enough to allow prices to reach new highs. That is as attractive a narrative as one really needs.

As a buttress to the logic of getting on the ladder, there is also a widely held view that underpins the current property-owning urge in the UK: that money spent on rent is money wasted. Notwithstanding the case for money paid in interest to the bank on a mortgage being in some way wasted, or that renting avoids the payment of a hefty, upfront stamp tax charge (in the UK at least) and promotes labour mobility, this feeling that rent is money wasted has a specific origin beyond an instinctive sense of unfairness towards *rentier* behaviour (landlords earning income without having to work) and possibly in an equally deep instinct that ownership (rather than just residency) means something in itself.

In the UK, one could argue that the point of departure for mass property ownership was the adoption of MITR (Mortgage Interest Tax Relief) in 1968, which made provisions for mortgage interest payments to be treated as tax deductible, thus providing an incentive to favour owner-occupation over renting. While this was essentially an incentive in terms of the cashflow concerns of the average household, its appeal was amplified by the relative cheapness of housing in the 1960s in terms of income to house prices, itself an incidental but critical factor. Particularly for middle-class and lower-income households, MITR made a profound difference with respect to the average family's decision to own rather than to rent, and has no doubt contributed to the widely held belief that renting is a waste of money. What is perhaps most interesting as a general observation about the reattribution of value and its *stickiness* is that MITR's later incarnation MIRAS (Mortgage Interest Relief at Source) was in fact finally abolished in April 2000, and with it the original cashflow incentive to own rather than rent. Despite this, the received wisdom of the benefit of ownership over rental is still a popular mantra.

The continued preference towards ownership may in part be due to the post-2000 period being one of falling interest rates, meaning the cashflow burden of mortgages in the UK became less onerous, particularly for those with memories of much-higher interest rates in the 1980s and 1990s (the UK base rate touched 17% in the early 1980s and then peaked again at 15% in September 1992). The bank bailouts following the global financial crisis (GFC) in 2008 meant the house-price crash was only a temporary blip and that bank lending could continue, albeit in a slightly more constrained manner due to banks being required to hold more capital against their loan books. The Bank of England's post-GFC monetary policy, characterised by low base interest rates, meant monthly mortgage payments stayed low. The combination of low inflation, accommodative monetary policy and a bail-out mentality encouraged risk taking and also assuaged any fear of downside losses to leveraged investments, of which property is one example.

One must also be aware of government tapping into the instinct for ownership and the feeling of self-worth and identity that comes with it, even if that self-worth has its origins in a collective understanding that ownership of property (and assets more generally) can act as a vehicle to promote one's social status. While not originally her policy, Margaret Thatcher's promotion of the Right-To-Buy for council tenants in the 1980s and, more recently, the institution of the Help-to-Buy policy by the Conservative-Liberal Democrat coalition in 2013, reflect an ongoing government-sponsored attempt to widen the basis of home ownership in the UK.

Even the names of the successive policies bely a transition in sentiment about the nature of the act of owning one's own house, from nudging a choice between renting and owning (through MITR), through the right to ownership (via Right-to-Buy policies) to the assumption of that right as normative, such that the financing and guaranteeing of the whole transaction is now done by the taxpayer, as has been characterised by the Help-to-Buy policy.

There is a sense here of symbiosis in which government policy cannot be seen exclusively as guiding behaviour in a pre-ordained way; legislation clearly progressed down a path that increasingly had its own gravitational pull, and this could only have been the case if the government were enabling something that the people already valued and therefore wanted to happen. One could also argue that the absence of any capital gains tax on the sale of primary residences in the UK created a unique and attractive tax-free gap into which the value of property in purely monetary terms could rise without constraint, even if higher house prices meant higher stamp-tax bills when buying new properties. In this sense, it is as important to consider where government does not intervene as it is to assess where it does.

The missing part of the story of rising house prices is the expansion of credit. While technological change and a more general rise in the standard of living created the potential for property to be more valuable, and government policy has reinforced this cultural shift, the real 'enabler' was the expansion of mortgage lending and of money via credit more generally. This is what has allowed the rising value of property to be expressed in price terms. Homeowners obviously understand how mortgages work, and yet there is a general lack of awareness about how banking regulation has been the key driver of house-price change, and this is not purely because banking regulation is 'boring' or complex. The rise in house prices has mirrored an overall rise in debt in the economy, and this can be seen in an overall rise in the size of bank balance sheets since the 1970s, a process reaching a hiatus just before the global financial crisis. The close link between credit expansion and house prices does not necessarily jive with the popular expressions of housing value, particularly the 'Location, Location, Location' mantra. 'Credit, Credit, Credit' isn't quite so catchy, nor is it necessarily as easily understood.

At the heart of the problem of explaining the real nature of the upward shift in house prices over the decades is the critical, complex and divisive question of money, the jobs that money performs in the economy and how the expansion or contraction of credit affects this. Questions about the choice of monetary system (if indeed it really is a choice), its effect on the perception of money and the role money plays in the economy is where the real story about the expression of value through changing house prices finds itself most clearly expressed.

With respect to the UK banking sector, The Bank of England's 1971 report *Competition and Credit Control* paved the way for the reduction of quantitative credit controls via the introduction of reserve-to-asset ratios (how much capital banks hold in reserve against their mortgage portfolios), which resulted in an explosion in lending in the 1970s[5].

Commercial banks were now able to enter the mortgage market with more competitive lending rates and less oner-ous deposit demands than those previously offered by the traditional building societies. Simply put, more could be lent on easier terms and for a smaller upfront deposit. Given the inflationary backdrop of the 1970s, it did not take long for the average homeowner to realise that house prices could rise even as the notional value of a mortgage stayed the same, and this was a good thing from their point of view. That the expansion of credit was a contributory factor to the inflation that was prevalent in that decade was probably not something the average property owner considered. Whether borrowers really *knew* about these rule changes with respect to bank lending or merely *felt* or *benefited from* their effects, the liber-alisation of the banking system and the provision of credit was the key vector for the sudden increase in house prices.

There was also a demographic factor at play, with the baby-boomer generation reaching the age where household forma-tion increased demand for housing, but supply and demand factors cannot alone explain the full extent of the rise in house prices (or, for that matter, the inflation of the 1970s more generally). What counted was that the moment when the revaluation of housing could be expressed to its fullness in terms of price had arrived.

For housing, easier credit merely provided the means by which this new consumption demand was facilitated and through which its value was expressed, and the ensuing price rises became part of a process of revaluation, which in time transformed our sense of housing from being a good (albeit one which was consumed over a long period of time and was thus tradeable) to something more like an investment. While taking out a mortgage to buy a house was nothing new, the provision of credit from the older building societies had been essentially conservative in terms of the amount of leverage and relatively onerous in terms of the interest charged. Liberalising the banking system and thereby making credit easier to come by (and therefore more socially acceptable) was essentially a new thing in this context. The long process of the financialisation of the housing market had begun. This emergent trend was in no small part encouraged by government policy over the ensuing decades, especially with respect to encouraging people to *think* of home ownership increasingly as an investment. That this whole period occurred against the backdrop of a global push towards freer trade, reduced capital controls and easier credit can be regarded as self-reinforcing, and in many ways the transformation of the UK housing market was just a part of the emerging financialisation of the global economy.

Yet, even as housing became a social issue (in terms of broadening the basis of home ownership rather than ending homelessness) and therefore a political one, 'innovations' in the mortgage market appeared and allowed more leverage, pushing prices further and, in so doing, further intensifying the cult of home ownership. This innovation within the mortgage market has led to interest-only mortgages and, at various points, mortgages greater in value than the assessed value of property against which the mortgage was written, as with the Northern Rock bank's infamous 125% mortgage offering, which marked a high-point in lending in the run up to the GFC. In this context, one might say that the concept of 'innovation' in mortgage lending is always and everywhere a byword for lending more to those less able to pay back the principal.

With an aging population, the latest iteration of innovation in lending has been the 'lifetime mortgage' for the elderly, a structure that greatly increases the possibility of a sale of the asset on the mortgage-holder's death. Although the small print on mortgages has always made it clear that one's house is at risk if one doesn't keep up repayments, repossession was never the intended outcome. Mortgage lending to the old means there is a much higher chance that a property is repossessed on the death of the mortgage holder, as the mortgage was not necessarily written with the intention that the borrower would live long enough to pay back all the principal. Such a structure confuses the idea of ownership and occupation, and by so doing somewhat ironically collapses the demarcation between renting and owning, which was the original point of departure for taking out a mortgage to buy a house in the first place.

In a similar way, the introduction of buy-to-let mortgages in the UK in 1996 accelerated the trend to treating property purely as an investment. The innovation of buy-to-let mortgages as a further driver of house prices, particularly since the equity in one property could be used as a deposit on another, has meant that home ownership has almost come full circle and is now arguably a tool of social exclusion rather than one of social mobility, especially for the young who are struggling to get 'on the ladder' due to high prices and the large initial deposits needed to secure a mortgage. Any residual link between the idea of house (as a durable good or physical asset) and home (as a medium of household formation) has been untethered, effectively creating a new rentier class, the consequences of which are now somewhat amorphously tied-up in the UK's current 'housing crisis' and the emergence of a 'generation rent'. It would seem then that innovation with respect to the provision of credit has increasingly allowed property values to reach their logical (or illogical) conclusion.

When one talks about a shortage of housing then, one has to be very careful when using arguments about insufficient numbers of dwellings to explain house-price appreciation of the past fifty years. In the UK at least, issues relating to green-belt restrictions or restrictive land-bank policies by house builders (where developers hold land and have planning permission to build on it but refrain from doing so to manage housing supply) do act as checks on supply. Immigration can affect the overall demand for housing in the economy. Changes to patterns of household formation (more, smaller households) also affect the demand for residences and for the type of dwellings required. Demography is obviously another issue, since people living longer reduces housing supply on a relative basis.

Yet to say that house prices will fall only if there are many more houses built is to conflate property supply and demand dynamics with the provision of and innovation in credit (the mortgage market) on the one hand and this additional trend towards treating housing as an investment on the other. More houses does not mean more affordable houses, at least not without government subsidies, and such subsidies generally maintain prices rather than reduce them. To claim that rising house prices are a product of insufficient supply and growing demand is a grossly inadequate and reductive explanation and one that ignores the credit and money aspect of the issue. There are those in the unfortunate position of being homeless or of being in temporary accommodation, but they are not really the people in question when the housing crisis issue is raised in the press or by politicians. A housing crisis that revolves around wanting more space, a different location or wanting to own rather than rent is really a crisis of aspiration, as it relates to a question of ownership and affordability rather than residency and occupation.

Given the greater financial (and emotional) capital newly invested in property, periods of falling house prices are made all the more unpleasant as the effect of financial leverage from borrowing via a mortgage amplifies losses just as it enhances returns, and behavioural economics suggests we feel the losses more than we do the gains[6]. The nature of the experience is a key factor here. In the UK, the combination of bank bailouts, rate cuts and then quantitative easing meant the housing crash during the global financial crisis of 2007–9 was short-lived enough not to leave any lasting damage on homeowners' (or debtors') psyches. This contrasts with the experiences of negative equity during the UK housing crash of the early 1990s.

Because the pound sterling was at the time tied to the Deutschmark due to Britain's membership of the European exchange-rate mechanism (ERM), UK interest rates had to be kept at a high level to keep the pound pegged within the designated currency band. These interest rates were inappropriately high for a domestic economy that was slowing and consequently wreaked havoc on household cashflows by pushing-up mortgage payments, resulting in defaults, repossessions and forced sales[7]. The pound eventually fell out of the ERM and, since this permitted lower interest rates more appropriate for the domestic economy, the subsequent recovery in house prices meant those who struggled but survived could look back on the period as just an episode within a longer-term beneficial upward move in property values. The situation of negative equity, where one's mortgage was greater than the value of one's house, became a distant memory. The subsequent rise in house prices suggests that the experiences of the early 1990s were clearly insufficient to disturb the British love affair with housing, at least in terms of dissuading new entrants from the market.

Elsewhere, much is made of how Japan's experience following the bursting of its bubble in 1990 will act as a script for other countries should they too end up experiencing a period of debt-deflation. Debt-deflation is a situation where the stock of debt is sufficiently high that the cost of servicing it becomes so onerous that it restricts overall consumer demand in the economy, leading to a general fall in prices. In Japan, house prices fell by more than half and remained depressed for thirty years. These falling asset prices (including falling house prices) were due to the bursting of a monstrous asset-price bubble at the end of the previous decade, and this bubble had been fuelled by rapid credit expansion by the banks, the property element of which was characterised by an intensity and frenzy that might even make the property-loving British blush.

The slow unwinding of the excess of debt after the bubble burst and the lack of demand for new borrowing during this period meant strong deflationary tendencies became embedded in Japanese economic expectations, including in house prices. These deflationary tendencies were arguably exacerbated by an aging population who consumed less, further reducing demand within the economy. House prices in Japan may never regain their nominal 1990 peak (absent a breakdown in the money system through hyperinflation or the like). But to describe to the average British homeowner how, with an aging population and following the bursting of a credit bubble, prices plummeted, never to recover, usually elicits a response of incomprehension mixed with attestations that somehow the UK market is inherently different and that it could never happen here[8].

There *are* differences between the housing markets in Japan and the UK. Since value is particular, markets tend to be idiosyncratic and some of the peculiarities of the Japanese housing market are critical to considering how the bubble grew and also the manner in which it burst. The Japanese have a hefty 4% tax on reregistering inherited property, meaning the bereaved are less keen to inherit. This can only be truer with an aging and shrinking population and one already accustomed to the loss-avoiding deflationary mindset. This contrasts with tax incentives in the UK such as the absence of capital gains being charged on primary residences when they are sold.

The Japanese tend to build new houses every twenty or thirty years, and this may limit the desirability of property inheritance by the younger generation from the old. Indeed, the ratio of new-build to second-hand housing in Japan of two to one is roughly the inverse of the UK[9]. In the UK, houses are houses, and often the oldest ones are the most desirable because of their location or 'character'. Perhaps this is just due to the choice of brick or stone over wood as the main building material in the UK, and the consequent age of much of the housing stock that results. Reflecting this, the very term 'second-hand housing' is something that seems alien to the language of the UK property market. Buying a 'second-hand' house does not have the same stigma attached to it that someone might suffer if they were some-what disingenuously labelled as 'only being able to afford a second-hand car'.

There are problems other than deflation and declining aggregate demand due to aging populations. During the 2017 general election campaign in the UK, the Conservative party, in a misguided attempt to garner popularity, focused their manifesto on bringing back fox-hunting and introducing a policy to increase the means-testing of care for the elderly. The latter was promptly branded a 'death tax' as it potentially involved the sale of housing assets to pay for nursing care that the deceased had previously received. Misguided or untimely, the proposal belied the growing problem of paying for the care of an aging population from a shrinking tax base. As the population continues to age, the pressure for similar policy proposals will endure.

In the context of people increasingly living well into their eighties, one way of looking at this issue is to ask how feasible it is not to work for twenty-one or twenty-two years (while one is being educated), then working for forty-five or so years, then not working for another twenty-odd years during retirement. This is a slightly stylised question – it isn't just a question of the individual's pension savings and assets or how much employers contribute to workers' pension schemes. There are clearly intergenerational commitments (parents have a financial responsibility for their children) while the taxpayer faces an ongoing burden to pay for education, healthcare and state-retirement benefits (in the UK at least). What is different now is the sheer number of people reaching retirement age and then going on to live for a few decades afterwards. At a national level, this is a historic first from the point of view of individuals, companies and the state.

Growing demand for domestic care for the elderly will likely lead to an increasing number of older homeowners seeking to extract money from their housing assets in what in the UK is called equity release (also known in the United States as the reverse mortgage). The very logic of saving is one driven by the need or desire to delay consumption, and retirement is the moment that delayed consumption comes due. If the monetary value in property is increasingly to be extracted for the purpose of retirement spending, what of house prices then?

Whether through government policies to place the burden of the cost of care for the elderly on the wealthy or through personal initiative to ensure a comfortable retirement, the focus on housing as the great, untapped source of wealth in the UK as the means to pay for the baby-boomers in retirement is well in train already. Either by choice or coercion, over time this process could result in a large proportion of the housing stock eventually having to be sold, as estates have to pay back the equity-release debt by selling the housing assets against which the equity was originally withdrawn by the deceased.

Were this to happen, it could mean that the UK experiences an extended period of falling house prices similar to the Japanese, driven by a similar demographic imperative of an aging population. This in turn begs the question, especially if house prices clear at a permanently lower level, whether the UK just experienced a fifty-year housing bubble, one that was so long yet so pervasive as to pass almost unnoticed except in its most egregious interludes. Suggesting that a fifty-year rise in house prices is not a bubble but the 'fundamentals of supply and demand' is of no consolation if one then suffers a Japanese-style thirty-year decline.

Should the UK struggle with a period of debt-deflation (whatever the proximate cause), one wonders how the perception of value in housing will change. Likewise, should the demographic demands of aging start to affect asset prices, the collective wisdom of home ownership may start to be questioned. For those who have invested in housing for their pensions, the act of *monetising* what is essentially a physical or non-monetary asset with no yield of its own (renting as a source of income from housing is an additional action and not one inherent to property ownership in its basic form of owner-occupation) either through sale or equity-release will likely put downward pressure on house prices. For younger generations priced out of the housing market and more used to renting, perhaps the value or appeal of property ownership itself will change. If the young, locked out of the housing market due to high house prices, increasingly value 'experiences' and the sharing of them (especially through social media) over the ownership of assets, why would they want to own a house if they could just rent? There may be a tendency or instinct towards ownership, but the degree to which it is expressed may moderate because of circumstances and differing life experiences.

Predicting how the reattribution of value will occur in the future is really just a matter of speculation. The slow-moving nature of the housing market, people's need for housing and general reluctance to default on their mortgages except as a final resort dampens price volatility in the housing market. For fixed-rate mortgage holders, there is lag between changes to central-bank interest rate policy and monthly mortgage payments as these only reset when the borrowing rate is refixed, which is generally every two to three years in the UK. In order to ensure stability in the banking sector, government and central bank policy has, over time, become increasingly focused on maintaining asset prices (or trying to reverse corrections), and market participants, including in the housing market, are of course incentivised by this. Because housing costs and house prices are a critical consideration for households, the housing narrative has considerable depth, from government, central banks, and the public at large. It is likely therefore that most are tightly wedded to their existing opinions and beliefs about the housing market (especially after a long and barely interrupted rise in prices) and therefore people will be disinclined to change their opinion or would only do so following a major exogenous shock.

One such shock could be an extended period of inflation, and here the issue about housing becoming an investment (and a leveraged one at that) starts to work against the long and successful story of rising house prices. While the rates on mortgages on US real estate tend to be fixed for twenty or thirty years, the UK tends to have long-dated mortgages but with much shorter-dated interest-rate fixes, the longest of which is usually only five years (although there are a few exceptions), while many are floating-rate contracts that track short-term interest rates. While short-dated fixed or floating-rate mortgages have been attractive in the low-interest-rate, disinflationary period following the global financial crisis, an extended period of inflation would, albeit with a time-lag as mortgages approach refinancing, start to work against borrowers if one assumes that higher inflation would lead to higher mortgage rates.

Thus, while a period of inflation might see homeowners in the US benefiting from capital appreciation to their houses even as their mortgages, fixed for up to thirty years, became more affordable in nominal terms, in the UK, with its shorter-term fixes, it is likely that rising mortgage rates would start to affect house prices in a more adverse manner. In a financialised world, it is the terms of credit that matter, not the asset against which the debt is held. The same is true of the legal standing of the borrower. Mortgages in the US tend to be non-recourse loans from which the borrower can walk away (hence the term 'jingle-mail' – the sound of the keys being posted back through the letter box by a departing mortgage defaulter). Borrowers in the UK have no such freedom and the mortgage debt is binding.

In that sense, while slow-burning issues like demography or debt-deflation may have already dictated the future pattern of the value of housing, one is just guessing at the where and when of future prices. If one is looking for historical analogies, not only is the list of examples for comparison generally limited in number, the legal, social, technological and cultural differences between these prior examples and the current case means the former do not provide a *model* for the latter. While previous examples can be used to illustrate the forces at work, they do not dictate the likely outcome of current events or their timing. If this is the case, this already falls far short of assuming the same causality, and this means we cannot rely on induction to discern a general process to predict future outcomes in the way we would normally with scientific experimentation.

Relying on historic price data from a discrete event or period to predict the future with any degree of certainty is an exercise in radical overconfidence, yet this practice is most commonplace in economic and market analysis. The formula is a simple one: 'the current situation is like [insert time period or event] because [insert reason]'. As the 2020s progress, global economic events may turn out to be a bit like the 1910s (deficit-driven inflation then depression), the 1930s (debt deflation and banking crises), the 1940s (high growth, high inflation but low bond yields due to central-bank intervention) or the 1970s (rising commodity prices, high unemployment and high inflation – better known as stagflation). Perhaps we will experience some or all of them, but pinning one's argument to a prior decade's experience is probably not the optimal way to proceed. The danger comes from the desire to look for patterns, itself a product of what Ludwig Wittgenstein described as a 'craving for generality' and a preoccupation with scientific method leading to a desire to explain natural phenomena with the minimum number of 'primitive natural laws'[10]. While this is natural enough for the analytic mind, it often overlooks the importance of ascertaining difference and idiosyncrasy, not least the observation that knowledge of prior events affects current ones.

Yet what seems to happen most often is a bland reliance on induction and the assumption that tomorrow will be very much like today. If one is bearish on property, for example, and believes that a secular shift is underway due to any number of reasons including inflation, debt-deflation or demographic pressures, one is currently making a strong statement about value but a weak one about price, especially if long-run prices have not really changed yet. Should one believe that an excess of debt inevitably leads to a deflationary collapse in prices, then what one is really saying is that the property crash has already happened but has yet to be reflected in house prices. If house prices have not yet collapsed, this would constitute a very personal or minority view of the value of housing – if the popular understanding of the value of housing started to reflect a view like this, only then would prices start to move.

*   *   *

In the UK, one explanation for the exceptionally high house prices in London and the South East (beyond the obvious point that London is a global hub of finance and so on) is the pervasiveness of the interest-only mortgage, where one pays just the interest on the loan rather than paying down the principal. As a mortgage product, this is a direct bet on higher house prices. The exceptional price rises in London housing have made interest-only a good bet – they also allow a much higher loan-to-value ratio, thereby gearing the housing market further, creating a loop of higher transaction prices and more housing wealth. Added to this, the housing market is one where there tends to be little profit-taking. Apart from the elderly down-sizing to a more manageable-sized dwelling, it is often the case that profits are effectively 'rolled-up' into a bigger sum of equity used to secure a correspondingly larger mortgage to fund the next acquisition. There is a certain practical logic to this, such as when households need more physical space as families grow in size, but it also reflects the role of housing as a source of social status. If, however, London house prices were to level out for any number of reasons (selling by older homeowners, more onerous taxation, rises in interest rates and so on), then those with large interest-only mortgages would face a singular problem: how do they pay down the principal?

This may not be an immediate problem, but it would become so at some stage, given the logic that interest-only mortgages require ever-rising house prices to function. The lower interest rate secured on interest-only mortgages generally allows a correspondingly higher level of borrowing for a given level of personal income. Servicing an equivalent size of amortising debt (i.e., paying interest and principal simultaneously) would be far more onerous using the same monthly household cashflow. If the property market looked as though it had settled at a plateau (i.e., not even lower, just at the same level) over a long enough time frame (such as Japan's thirty-year hiatus), many would eventually have to sell when they retired, depressing prices. The very effect of debt growing through time via compounding demands that leveraged asset prices rise too, otherwise there is a solvency crisis. Looked at from this perspective, it is hard to distinguish the cult of house prices from the cult of debt.

*   *   *

At various points in the last forty years, the government has encouraged people to save for retirement through investing in housing. This seems a little back-to-front, as buying a property most often means taking out a mortgage and therefore one is in fact borrowing, not saving. When we talk about our pension savings, we talk about how we invest the money we have, yet at the same time when companies make capital investments or investment takes place in the economy at large (including in the public sector), it somehow feels as if something different is happening, even if the word we use, *investment*, is the same.

This linguistic problem can be explained through the link between investment and debt. Saving is an act undertaken in the present with a view to the future, and investment is the means by which we (or companies or governments) choose to do that. One should not be confused by any issue of agency: I may save by depositing my excess earnings in a bank and the bank may then in turn lend money to a business to build a new factory, say, but my saving and the banking lending need not both happen. I just happen to be investing my savings in a deposit account; but banks can lend without deposits from savers, thus investment can be facilitated through the use of debt. One can borrow to invest, either from domestic sources or abroad, the latter being the case where overall investment in the economy exceeds the saving rate.

We have a binary choice – to consume (an action in the present for the present) or to save (an action in the present with a view to the future), but we can use credit to do both if we want or need to. There is a particular meaning of the word *investment* that makes it feel different to saving (such as when a company invests in plant or research-and-development), but both my saving in a deposit account and the company's investment are actions in the present with a view to the future. Another way of looking at this is by saying my investing in the shares of a particular company that then in turn invests in a new factory are temporally equivalent acts of saving, differing only in the form the investment takes.

While borrowing for consumption is effectively *dis*saving, in the sense that the repayment of debt in the future reduces future consumption, borrowing to invest is, by contrast, *leveraged* saving – saving more than one initially has using debt. When a company invests, it can do so from retained earnings or by issuing equity or debt. Likewise, a government can invest using tax receipts or by running a deficit funded by borrowing. Buying a house using a mortgage is no different in terms of the financial transaction itself. The key point is the temporal aspect of investment with respect to saving as an action in the present with a view to the future. The source of the funds is, in a sense, irrelevant to the act of investing itself.

There was no issue when housing was essentially just a good, not an investment, but a confusion arises if one is both consuming (housing as a good) and delaying consumption (housing as an investment and a means of saving) in the same action. Compounding this quirk is the very nature of housing as an asset that yields nothing. Those who rent out properties do just that: they are landlords of some sort, not mere owner-occupiers. Houses on their own pay no dividends or coupons, and thus seem an odd choice of investment vehicle for the would-be retiree who eventually needs to draw down his or her savings in order to pay the bills. The problem with a good becoming an investment (as housing has become) is the issue of *realising* the monetary value of what is essentially a non-monetary asset. This is a problem of the *why* of economics raised in the previous chapter; if you are saving for retirement, then doing so by buying a house may seem smart as house prices rise, but less so if everyone is in the same boat and will have to monetise their investment at a similar age and for the same reason.

In terms of realising value, housing is a highly illiquid investment, as it cannot really be sold in parts, and even equity release (reverse mortgaging in the US) ultimately necessitates a sale of the entire property if the loan principal cannot be repaid by another means. Monetary inflation in terms of a growth in credit explains much of how housing transformed from something that was largely a good into something which is now a hybrid between a good and an investment. One can see here the grounds on which a revaluation could work the other way; perhaps Japan's experience (of both deflation and demographic aging) shows the way back again. But this is not to say that everything ought to be thought of as a cycle; credit itself changes the nature of ownership and what it means, and thus the next iteration of value may well be decidedly different and in a new form. This seems particularly likely given the growing importance of environmental considerations with respect to social and economic planning. The green transition might, for example, see large price discounts appear for those houses with worse insulation or higher energy consumption as government regulation becomes more onerous and intrusive.

*　　*　　*

Why does the question about whether housing is a good or an investment matter? Behind these somewhat arbitrary terms and the economic decisions reflected in them is the question of the health of the economy and the wellbeing of the society in which it functions. Goods and services are for consumption and investments are for saving. When that gets confused, lower economic growth can be the product, and this is not so much the fault of the individual economic agents concerned but of the specific economic structure in question, particularly its money system and how that affects the stock of debt within the economy and what that debt is used for. Borrowing for investment is key to growth in the economy, while borrowing to consume has the opposite effect, as growing interest payments choke future consumption, depressing economic activity. Can we really say definitely whether mortgage holders are borrowing to invest or just borrowing to consume? Do they even know that this is *a* choice rather than *the* choice?

What is clearer is that, unlike bonds (which pay coupons) or shares (which pay dividends), property of itself is an asset with no yield. The need to monetise what is an essentially physical asset could create a situation in which houses prices could become depressed due to selling, which in turn could disturb the stability of the mortgage debt markets. This very idea of leveraged investment in property – the idea of borrowing (via a mortgage) in order to save for one's retirement – could also arguably be siphoning off savings that could be invested more productively elsewhere in the real economy. This is in addition to the idea that servicing the sort of large mortgages that are needed to afford high house prices reduces the money available for debtors to spend on consumption elsewhere, which is a potential long-term source of deflation and low growth. Clearly, high property valuations come at a price and the transformation of property-as-good into property-as-investment has many potential consequences.

Good economics knows the limits of its claims, and economic history, particularly the focus on difference and idiosyncrasy, is a vital tool in establishing these limits. If the basic choice in economics is one between consumption and saving, the conclusion from this examination of the UK housing market and the expansion of debt that has accompanied it should be that borrowing to consume is bad for an economy as debt-servicing weighs on consumption and growth, while borrowing to invest is the key to economic progress. So much is clear, but when one has to ask in any particular example what is a good and what is an investment (as has this discussion) and, therefore, what actually constitutes consumption and what is saving, then the limit to economics' claim to generality start to appear. The next step in analysing these limits is to examine more closely our perception of value.

Beneath this narrative about the nature of the UK housing market in the last half century or so there have been two concurrent themes: those of the dynamic nature of value on the one hand and of the role of credit and its effect on the money supply (through monetary inflation) on the other. Earlier in the chapter, value was described as a somewhat amorphous idea. This is in part because it is dynamic, something that is constantly changing, but also because it is clearly not just a number or an amount, even if it is often represented as such.

The discussion above suggests that by the second half of the twentieth century, a series of factors had come together to make houses more liveable, and that people had more leisure time to spend in them and more overall wealth (in terms of rising standards of living) to make them better symbols of self-expression or social standing. While value in some circumstances can be reduced to a number (in terms of money), there is clearly more to value than just this reductive calculation. The next chapter therefore examines how things become *valuable*, and this in turn is really a question of how we value things. Much of economics starts with the idea of a price as being something true. Prices are certainly real in the sense that they are the empirical data of economics but, by using value and valuation rather than price as a point of departure, one isn't bound to an economic world of fixed rules where historic price trends are analysed as certain guides to the future. Rather than seeking empirically true statements about price, the goal is to examine more closely the dynamic nature of value and how value *relates* to price.

3.

FOR WHAT IT'S WORTH: THE NATURE OF VALUE

One of the more peculiar inventions in economics is the idea of *homo economicus* or 'economic man'. This hyper-rational being has yet to be updated for the twenty-first century into something with less gender bias (perhaps *persona economica* would be more appropriate) but, this issue notwithstanding, the individual in question is rational, profit maximising, always seeking maximum utility from economic interactions and reacting immediately (and in a rational fashion) to changes in information. This invention is a product of a way of thinking with its origins in the logical chain that starts with prices and works backwards from there to discern patterns in economic behaviour. Prices are the empirical facts of economics and act as a record of our interactions in the economic sphere. If one can discern a pattern in prices, one can discern a schema of action that predicts how people will react to changes (say, in supply or demand) and, from this, one can start building a theory of economic action.

However, it only takes a cursory glance at the gyrations of the stock market to suspect that this inflexible rationality is a little unrealistic. More recently, behavioural economics has tried to reappraise this assumed economic rationalism by showing how much of our economic decision-making is irrational – or at least not logically rational in the purely numeric sense of profit maximisation. In his 2011 book, *Thinking Fast and Slow*, Daniel Kahneman suggested that there are in fact two types of system in the mind. The first is the impulsive, quick-fire emotional response to one's environment and the other a slower, more deliberative approach that might generally be called 'cerebral'. Depending on our experience and circumstances, we may react in a Type 1 manner (emotional and impulsive) or a Type 2 manner (rational and deliberative)[1].

While on the one hand *homo economicus* is an eminently rational being and on the other the experiments of behavioural economists tend to show that utility and rational profit-maximisation are not always the outcome of the actions of economic agents, both tend to use questions of price as a point of departure. Some of the behaviouralist experiments simply highlight how poor we are at mental arithmetic, especially when calculations relating to compound interest are involved. Biases and heuristics (rules-of-thumb) abound in our decision-making. Even if one uses Kahnemann's Type 1 (fast/emotional) and Type 2 (slower/cerebral) distinction, there is still a question about whether one really knows at any given moment how one is thinking. Aside from examining one's brain patterns to see what part of the brain 'lights up' when presented with certain problems, the only way one really knows whether one is thinking in Type 1 or Type 2 mode is to ask oneself that very question at any given moment. Not only is this distinctly Type 2 behaviour, it is also something that one is unlikely to do if one is really putting one's mind to something in a thoroughly Type 2 way.

An alternative approach to the problem of how we think about economic decision-making that bypasses the rational/irrational debate is to examine more closely the way we simply talk about economic affairs and what we mean when we use certain expressions. This is particularly useful if one is using the idea of value as a point of departure rather than price. Rather than looking at price series and the patterns involved in them and working backwards to find out what that means in terms of decision-making (rational or otherwise), by looking at what we value and how we express that in linguistic terms, we can hope to ascertain new knowledge about how we come to economic decisions. Implicit in this is the idea that economic action – buying and selling – is the thing that creates prices. Looking at price first and creating a model of human action based on this is back-to-front. An alternative is to look at how our sense of value and what we value changes, and how this then manifests itself in price, based on the idea that a change in our sense of value drives us to the economic activity of buying and selling, and price is the outcome of the transaction resulting from this.

For a close examination of the language that we ordinarily use when talking about economic affairs and what we mean when talking in this way, it is necessary to use some of the techniques of linguistic philosophy. The basic idea of philosophy of language is that the best (and only) way to come to a theory of knowledge is through a theory of language and that the tools of linguistic philosophy are those most suitable for establishing what we mean when we use ordinary language[2]. This isn't a question of linguistics or etymology, but more about how the sense we get from our ordinary use of language provides a meaning for the terms used. This will be especially useful for the idea of value, itself a term with many applications. By understanding better what value means, it is possible to start to see what makes valuation a dynamic process, and from this we can link value to price in what is perhaps the correct order (i.e., changes in value cause changes in price) rather than the back-to-front fashion implicitly embedded in much current economic theory (price is an empirical truth, and we can infer a meaning from that, be it rational or irrational).

As a starting point for an analysis of value, it is worth noting that the term crops up repeatedly in the language of economics and the financial markets. We talk about deep value, intrinsic value, fundamental value, of value traps, of assets being over- and under-valued and so on. More broadly, we talk about moral values, family values, even of senti-mental value. If one is looking to make general propositions about value, one really needs to start by examining to what extent values are shared phenomena and how what we value individually (for example the sentimental value of a particular object) relates to that which is valued more generally (such as housing, as illustrated in the previous chapter), if at all. The question here is whether or when individual interests become shared or common interests, and how that is expressed in language.

In his aphorism 'meaning is use', the philosopher Ludwig Wittgenstein asserted that the meaning of words comes from how we ordinarily use them rather than from a fixed definition[3]. The role words play in everyday language exchanges (or *language games* in Wittgenstein's terminology) dictates what we mean by them, and this process is a collective one, since language functions as a shared tool. If one for example asks what the difference is between a collector and a hoarder, it isn't just that a certain image or sense is created in one's mind, but that we are aware of how we would normally use these words and what we would mean by using them in this way. It is immediately clear from our ordinary use of language that we feel that there must be some value in what the collector collects but not in what the hoarder hoards. This seems true even without knowing what the object of the collecting or hoarding actually is. If anything, it doesn't matter what the hoarder hoards, since the hoarder's stash has to be of a random or inexplicable nature, not only by any conventional measure of value but also because of how we employ the word in speech or writing.

We tend to think of something as being collectable if we already consider it to be worth keeping. By contrast, hoarding is not just the private activity of collecting what most people think of as worthless tat; the term also has connotations of excess and therefore of being intrinsically anti-social or even asocial, perhaps reflecting some stigma at the origins of the urge to hoard in mental trauma of some kind. Dragons hoard gold, and at the start of the recent pandemic, some people hoarded toilet paper. The hoarders of useless tat perhaps get treated a little unfairly in this context. They may well prove at some point to have been no more than untimely collectors; it could be that after enough time has passed, an aggregation of the seemingly worthless detritus of the everyday can acquire an allure all of its own. The interior design industry, for example, thrives on the reanimation and reuse of the once-discarded, often under the guise of 'retro chic' or something similar, and invariably for a tidy profit. Over time, we may start to appreciate that rare phenomenon of someone having once valued that which everyone else took for granted, even if their hoarding was compulsive. In addition, one ought not to confuse the hoarder and his or her hoarding with the hoard itself as a thing; the unearthed treasure hoard provides a totally different sense to the word from that which one gets when talking about the activity of hoarding. A hoard in this context denotes a legal term used in the context of establishing proper ownership for what might broadly be termed as archaeological discoveries[4].

More generally, though, we tend to see some point in what the collector does, even if the collection in question has no intrinsic utility. If anything, the more impressive and extensive the collection, the lower the utility of it to the collector; this seems particularly true for the collector of things like cars, which by their nature can only be driven one at a time.

By contrasting the use of the word *collector* with that of *hoarder*, the manner in which we attribute economic value is revealed. Its genesis may lie in utility, but that is neither necessary nor sufficient for a definition; utility demands the context of time and place. Something may be useful now or useful in the future, and the degree of value in this utility varies as a consequence. In this respect, the contrast between collecting and hoarding might start to reveal the frontier between consumption and saving and, in so doing, show how the attribution of value is a process that acquires meaning only in time. One might ask of a hoarder, 'Why do you need so much of this now?' or, 'Why are you keeping so many of those for the future?' and in so doing show that the hoarder is not following some currently accepted convention for consuming and saving. The intimation of excess within our use of the word *hoarder* does not so much reflect the breach of a fixed level of consumption or saving but that it is not what *we* would do or feel is acceptable now.

Beyond its aesthetic appeal, a collection of fine artworks has a utility of sorts, if that utility is seen through the medium of signifying social status or wealth. We recognise some value in the activity of the collector that is absent from the activity of the hoarder, and this is the same as saying we value what the collector collects but not what the hoarder hoards.

Value in an economic sense, therefore, only acquires meaning within a shared social context and, while it is not necessarily a standard, it clearly has normative qualities, particularly since collecting is a choice while hoarding has the appearance of being a compulsion. There is no value or valuation in nature – it is we who value the natural world for its own beauty or who value the resources it provides. Yet, since we as humans use the resources of the natural world for our survival, one could say ecology stops where economics starts, the latter being an entirely human endeavour, and increasingly one that seems to put the natural world in peril.

Value is therefore not an additional quality that things can possess beyond our finding them valuable. To say that people value things is to describe the very nature of economics rather than to describe a separate activity within it. The sense of what we mean here is that we have found this thing valuable in the past, do so in the present and believe we will likely do so in the future, all else being equal. We share with the collector a sense of purpose in the act of collecting. The attribution of value is therefore a purposive social endeavour, linking the past to the future through an ongoing activity in our present. This works both ways insofar as value can fall as well as rise.

When economics is described in terms of the allocation of scarce resources, the idea of scarcity here is an expression of value. If finding things to be of value for this reason is considered as a shared human activity, then the scope of the economic sphere is also defined by the same criteria. What is important to note here is that this does not assume that all that lies within the economic sphere is valued in monetary terms. One way of explaining what we really mean when saying something has intrinsic value (value in itself) would be to say that some things have a value to us that is not best expressed in monetary terms even if it is significant within the economic sphere. Indeed, the encroachment of money into new areas of our daily life is neither new, nor surprising, nor necessarily desirable. Thomas Carlyle's critique of the 'cash nexus' in a pamphlet of 1839, in which he felt money was increasingly depersonalising all economic interactions, is no different to the view of those in England who opposed the gradual financialisation of the higher education system in the form of university tuition fees from 1997 onwards[5]. Education clearly has an impact on productivity and therefore on economic growth, but its benefits should not only be understood merely as a factor in the growth of gross domestic product (GDP). The point here is that we talk about value and what things are worth – to measure value in terms of money is just one instance of this, albeit, through habit and happenstance, the dominant one.

*   *   *

A key tool in behavioural economics is the use of games and roleplaying and the analysis of trends in the subsequent interactions. Players come together in scenarios and create markets where theoretical transactions occur. There is no physical marketplace or stock exchange – the very coming together in the game or scenario itself is the market being created. One of the most prescient and enduring observations by Adam Smith in *The Wealth of Nations* is the benefits that accrue from the specialisation of labour[6]. Markets are *events* in which competing interests are reconciled but whose relative efficiency and mutual benefit increases with the divergence and variety of the participants' skills and knowledge in relation to the overall aggregate of needs and desires. This is another reason to dismiss the idea of *homo economicus* and the theorising that

comes from the approach of arguing about rational expectations. The idea of homo economicus *stepping into* a market
to pursue his interest is flawed, and borrows too much from
the idea of a physical marketplace rather than seeing that the
market is made by the very act of economic agents coming
together.

If markets don't just exist but are *made* by those participat-
ing in them, then they must be predicated on the concept of
plurality. This is the case not only for goods and services, but
also ideas; the ancient Greek agora (marketplace) was a place
for critical debate as well as for trade[7]. In this context, the
model of homo economicus discussed earlier in the chapter
can therefore be rendered flawed on two further accounts.
First, because its point of departure is singular in number
not plural; the minimum it takes to make a market is two
people. Based on the idea that it takes at least two to tango
in a market, one necessarily needs to think relatively – of
the relations between market participants – not primarily of
the interests or the point of view of a single, hypothetical
individual. Secondly, and consequent to the first objection,
homo economicus as an abstract and theoretical entity sits
in the third person singular when, in fact, markets only exist
when we (first-person plural) or they (third-person plural)
make them.

This is another reason to favour the particular over the
general in economics: any particular *we* or *they* that constitutes a market does so at a particular time and in a particular
place, and this in itself gives the market a historical, social
and cultural context, which is unique, or at least which has

characteristics that distinguish it even from its close relatives. Markets function when there is both enough to bring people together in a community of shared interests (and values) and yet enough to mark them apart as individuals in terms of specific needs or desires at any particular moment.

By starting an analysis of the economic sphere in the plural rather than in the singular, the nature of the market as a shared endeavour is established from the outset. One implication of this is that the market system is better understood as much by its inherent collaboration as it is by competition for the best deal. While the transactional process of the marketplace itself is necessarily adversarial, our economic value system is a shared one, even if the degree to which each of us values the particular differs. Transactions in the marketplace create prices, and prices provide a record of the way in which our value of the particular changes through time.

What we value changes over time, as does the extent to which we value it. Eventually, these changes make themselves felt in prices. Of course, the speed at which value is reflected in price varies; prices in equities or bonds move almost instantaneously, in part because they are homogeneous (all common equity shares, for example, are by nature the same in terms of their legal claim) and can be listed on an exchange that has continuous pricing. The price of a particular house or piece of land only changes when it is transacted upon. This is irrespective of whether its value has risen or fallen in the meantime. What needs to be established is the correct characterisation of the relationship between value and price and how changes in the former result in changes to the latter. The point of departure, though, is value, not price.

According to the physicist Lord Kelvin, 'When you can measure what you are speaking about, and express it in numbers, you know something about it; but when you cannot measure it, when you cannot express it in numbers, your knowledge is of a meagre and unsatisfactory kind'[8]. This being so, it is understandable how economics tends to start with the numeric comfort blanket of price. If, on the other hand, one starts with value rather than price, one is as much in the realm of ordinary language as one is in the realm of numbers, however unsatisfactory this might initially seem with respect to Kelvin's assertion about precision.

Prices are facts while valuation is an activity the significance of which comes from a shared social context whose meaning is brought to bear through written or verbal discussion. Conversations about value are, however, often dominated by money. This is because money is, by convention, used as a measure of value as well as a record of price. To understand the difference between money-as-value and money-as-price is the first step in understanding the relationship between value and price and how the two stand in relation to one another in time. This relationship is best understood through looking at money as a single medium, which has to perform several functions at once.

Examining price series and discerning statistical patterns and relationships from them is a key part of the economist's job. If on the other hand one starts with value (rather than price), one is as much in the realm of ordinary language as one is in the realm of numbers. This is where the tools of linguistic philosophy come into their own: the close analysis of language to try to discern sense and meaning, but also to illustrate and hopefully clear up confusions caused by the shortcoming of language itself, and particularly the often vague or confusing way in which it is used.

In order to discern the relationship between value and price, and particularly how the two can be confused, a useful exercise is to compare and contrast how we variously talk about money as a measure of value and as a record of price. The four sentences below are illustrative of how monetary amounts can act fairly seamlessly as expressions of value as well as descriptions of price. That they concern housing is to a certain extent incidental, although it would seem appropriate to start with something that people actually love talking about.

1. 'I paid £1,000,000 for this house.'

2. 'My house is worth £1,000,000.'

3. 'My house is worth more than the £1,000,000 I paid for it.'

4. 'I hope to sell my house for more than the £1,000,000 I paid for it.'

Sentence 1 is a description of a completed and settled transaction in the past. Here, the £1,000,000 is a price and as such is an empirical fact. Sentences 2 and 3 are essentially subjective opinions on valuation occupying the present tense. In Sentence 2, the £1,000,000 is a measure of value; in Sentence 3, the value referred to is purely linguistic (i.e., 'more than' rather than a specific amount). Sentence 4 looks to the future, although there is clearly a degree of modality or possibility here ('Were I to find a buyer willing to pay what I think my house is now worth, then I shall sell it for more than the £1,000,000 I paid for it.'). As such, while the £1,000,000 refers to a historical price, the speaker is anticipating a new, higher price being made at some point.

1. 'I paid £1,000,000 for this house.'

In Sentence 1, the price constitutes a real, discrete event. Depending on the nature of the transaction, it is recorded on a land registry (for property), a company registry or stock exchange (for a security) or on a till receipt (for groceries). A price is the result of a buyer and seller coming together to make a bargain. If a series of transactions show rising prices, it is empirically true to say for example that 'house prices are going up', the inference being that the assets in question are equivalent or at least similar enough for the observer to group them as a meaningful category. A similar process of ellipsis (or extension through omission of detail) happens in terms of valuation when people observe that food prices are going up and so on. One need not know the price of every item in a supermarket to understand what someone means when they say that food is becoming dearer.

4. 'I hope to sell my house for more than the £1,000,000 I paid for it.'

In Sentence 4, the figure I have in mind is effectively my view of the price yet to be, should I find a willing buyer with whom I can agree a bargain. It is what I think someone will pay for the house, but it is nonetheless *my* sense of value, not the buyer's. The decision to sell is also an expression of value – perhaps I need to move for work or need a house with another bedroom for a newly arrived child – but these are essentially non-numeric expressions of value, not being directly considered here. An interested buyer will have a bid price in mind reflecting respectively his or her sense of value.

A transaction is an agreement resulting in a bargain, which produces a price. When transacting, it is necessary that we agree on price, but not that we agree on value. In fact, other than in a (theoretical) state of perpetual equilibrium, buyers will always see the value driving a transaction as increasing or at least staying the same in the future while sellers will see it falling or at best staying the same over time. (There are exceptions here, such as the hedger or forced seller, but considerations such as exogenous shocks forcing sales should be considered in the context of a general fall in value and therefore in price.)

A price is the product of a transaction that results from a *disagreement* about the value of the object in question. This is as true for major transactions (such as the purchase of a house or even a whole company) as it is at a trivial level. In terms of satiating my thirst, a bottle of water is more valuable to me than it is to the retailer whose shop I am in and whose stock is constantly depreciating towards a sell-by date. The shared, social nature of value is revealed by the very event of coming together to effect a transaction for a particular thing at a certain point; both buyer and seller must value the object or instrument in some way. There are some instances, such as corporate bankruptcy, where the value of a company's equity goes to zero with no transactions occurring to reflect this. Often it is the case that shares of listed companies are suspended before they can actually trade to zero. In this instance, a share 'price' of zero is a measure of value but not a price actually created from a bargain.

2. 'My house is worth £1,000,000.'

Sentence 2 is a pure statement of value and, as such, is not related to price in any way. It is really just a subjective opinion. I may have bought the house long ago at a price that only makes sense when adjusted for time and inflation, hence my new opinion about its current value. I may have inherited the property and therefore never had to transact to acquire legal title. Although Sentence 2 is strictly a subjective opinion in the first person, for it to make any sense, it has to stand up to the common context of the market. For example, if the house in question forms part of a terrace of similar houses, one of which has just sold for £250,000, then my declaration that my near-identical residence is worth four times as much is clearly absurd or just very wishful thinking. Should the house next door have sold for a cool £1,000,000 last week, Sentence 2 would seem quite reasonable within the accepted conventions of property valuation. Implicit here is the proximity of price to value in terms of time. The more frequent the price creation, the more certain the current market value.

Given how infrequently a particular house changes hands, it seems quite practical when assessing housing values to look at recent transactions for similar properties in the same area. Without a standardised or commoditised market, value is essentially local. Some of the confusion that arises between the idea of money-as-value and money-as-price stems from the varying degree of commoditisation and standardisation of the various goods and services available in an economy. It also derives from how often prices are formed. While one may feel strongly about the cost of a pint of milk if inflation is squeezing one's disposable income, this is different to having strong opinions about the *value* of that same pint differing markedly from one day to the next, unless one's consumption habits suddenly change (say I find out I am lactose intolerant and stop drinking milk in my tea altogether and the value of milk to me becomes negligible). The more idiosyncratic the object and the less frequent transactions in it (or in similar things), the less closely past prices can confirm current market value. This is not to say value is any less real than price – in a housing boom it feels as though all houses are worth more, irrespective of whether all houses actually change hands. The attribution of value is the shared element; the creation of prices through transactions is specific to the individuals involved and the particular asset in question.

3. 'My house is worth more than the £1,000,000 I paid for it.'

Sentence 3 is a statement of value and clearly reflects the perception that value and price are no longer the same. Perhaps my neighbour has just sold his almost identical property for a price far in excess of what I paid for mine. Perhaps the economy is booming and the ensuing feel-good factor means we sense that housing ought to perform strongly in terms of future transactions. The causality is not a given, although its sense is clearly that something has caused its value to rise – in my opinion, at least. While the attribution of value is something we do in the present with an eye to the future, it is usually based on our own past experience. Value and memory (or the lack of it) are intrinsically linked.

Sentence 3 also helps to show the temporal difference between price and value. Prices are necessarily historic, while the value is an opinion held by an individual in the present with a view to the future. Sentence 3 only makes sense if there is the possibility of a future transaction that allows a hoped-for value to be realised. If something can never be sold, its economic value in this context is nil. In such a situation, ownership may, however, continue for personal or psychological reasons. This is what we mean by sentimental value, a phrase often prefixed by the adjectival phrase 'only of'. If something is of sentimental value only, its economic value in a shared, social sense has ceased to exist. This sort of behaviour, when taken to excess, might indicate the psychological origin of hoarding as discussed above.

While it may simply be a symptom of the growing complexity, specialisation and co-dependence in society that has evolved over the centuries, there is a sense that more and more parts of life have started to fall within the realm of money-as-value and as such are primarily measured in monetary terms. There is, for example, an increasing tendency in tertiary education to think of the benefits of a degree in terms of future earnings power for the individual or for the uplift to economic growth for society as a whole rather than to think in terms of the joy of learning for its own sake, even if some still hold such ideals dear.

In a highly differentiated, globalised and *financialised* world, it may just be that it is easier to express things in monetary terms as we 'know what that means'. Habit or necessity (or both) may have made money into a kind of pecuniary equivalent to the global English (Globish) that allows simple, if not very deep, communication between people of differing nationalities whose first language is not English. In terms of the number expression of money itself (£1,000,000 etc), the near-universality of Arabic numerals and Indian place-value notation could be the means by which money-as-value has gained its dominant status[9]. Clearly there are myriad expressions of value which are non-monetary, and also things in society which cannot be reduced to a price (or if they are, lose their meaning and thus their real value). What is being stated here is how useful, easy, and thus universal it is to express value in monetary terms.

1. 'I paid £1,000,000 for this house.'
2. 'My house is worth £1,000,000.'

Sentences 1 and 2 illustrate how a shared system of counting can create confusion between price and value. The £1,000,000 in Sentence 1 refers to a real monetary balance now sitting in the bank account of the seller after the money has been debited from my own bank account. It reflects an event in the past (a legally binding, settled transaction). The £1,000,000 in Sentence 2 amounts to the same as 1 in terms of counting and is real in the sense that I believe it to be the case, but it is nonetheless a subjective statement about value rather than an objective statement about price. Unlike price, valuation resides in the present, not the past.

4. 'I hope to sell my house for more than the £1,000,000 I paid for it.'

When we talk about 'house prices going up', we mean both a general rise in the level of the prices of houses that have recently been bought and sold but, at the same time, we imply a likely rise in value for other properties that have not changed hands, and that this trend will continue. Once again, a shared system of accounting for price and value blurs our thinking about past and future. This temporal difference between price and value is further illustrated by Sentence 4. The modality (the possibility of an event happening) expressed here shows that value may not or may never be realised in the future[10]. In order that a bargain can be made at some point in the future, the assumption is that for every seller at a given offer price there must be a buyer who sees an equal or higher future value than that.

The concept of market liquidity is best illustrated in terms of the relationship between price and value. There are some instances where the value is nil. In terms of companies, the accounting concept of *going concern* could be described as the ability of a firm to generate cashflows sufficient to meet its financial and operational obligations on an ongoing basis. In this context, insolvency means that not only can a company not do this from its operations, but that there is no one willing to step in to offer credit to the firm even on an overnight basis; it literally will not survive the night and is thus economically dead. The firm's assets may yet be sold off and the creditors may receive partial compensation, but that is a separate matter. What is important here is that because there is no value to the equity, there can be no price to it either.

To effect a transaction, both parties must agree that there is some value to the asset. The strength of opinion about whether the value will rise or fall in the future dictates how much the buyer and seller are willing to transact at a given price. (This is true for both the amount of goods and services or the amount of money to be transferred, providing one believes that high prices not only mean high value but also a high-level conviction about value.) Liquidity is thus a measure of the degree of willingness with which market participants express their *implicit disagreement* with one another about value. The more they disagree, the more they are willing to trade or transact at a certain price. This is not just true of markets for listed financial securities, but is also the case for the overall number of transactions in the housing market, for example.

For a bargain to be made, therefore, necessarily market participants at the margin must agree on price but disagree on value. This is why trading volumes in financial markets are often lowest at the very top of a rally or the bottom of a sell-off but also highest when price moves are at their largest. During market peaks and troughs, there are fewer people to disagree with at a high level of conviction, be it bullish or bearish. The very event of a huge market rally or a precipitate sell-off suggests that too many people had to have been in agreement about value being too low (for a sharp rally to happen) or too high (in the case of a large sell-off). In a similar way to which the concept of homo economicus was critiqued earlier as an abstract and unrealistic 'third-person singular' view of the world, so liquidity as a concept is better understood in the plural than the singular. All too often, liquidity, particularly in financial markets, is analysed in terms of what *I* can buy or sell at a given time without adversely affecting the price. High levels of market volatility, characterised by sharply moving prices relative to overall market volume, are suggestive of low levels of conviction that the present level of valuation is 'right'. Good liquidity, characterised by high trading volumes amidst low relative price volatility, is a function of strong conviction about value but also strong disagreement about what that value is.

    1. 'I paid £1,000,000 for this house.'

    2. 'My house is worth £1,000,000.'

    3. 'My house is worth more than the £1,000,000 I paid for it.'

Sentences 2 and 3 are both expressions of value. In terms of parsing, they are in the first-person present tense ('I think that my house is worth . . .'). Sentence 1 looks ostensibly to be first-person past tense, although implicit in the logic of the transaction having happened is that it is plural, in that a buyer and seller must have agreed a price. The temptation, therefore, is simply to dismiss value as a subjective personal opinion, with all the ensuing biases that involves, not least that we would always like that which we have to be worth more than what we paid for it (the endowment theory). However, suppose we modify Sentence 3 as follows:

    3' 'The estate agent said my house is worth more than the £1,000,000 I paid for it.'

The sense in 3' is the same as that in 3 in that the perceived value now exceeds the price paid, but I am merely the beneficiary of an optimistic opinion on valuation, courtesy of a third-party. Whether that value is realised in the future through a transaction that produces a price is not relevant to who makes the valuation. A valuation is meaningful to the particular context in which it is expressed.

✳   ✳   ✳

The discussion above shows how we talk about value, how we impute worth and how prices fit into this schema of valuation. Trying to define what value means is a task that seems to bring up many of the same sort of complications encountered in philosophy of language when asking whether a particular proposition is true nor not. A number of parallels can be drawn between what we mean by the word *value* (valuable) and what we mean by the word *truth* (true)[11]. The list below looks at four different analytic definitions of truth: coherence, correspondence, utility and popularity. The principal analogies between value and truth are as follows:

1. **Intrinsic value / coherence theory of truth.** We might suggest that such-and-such is valuable for reasons inherent in the nature of the object itself. That people have continued to think of gold as money over time would be an example of this. The sort of properties that make gold into money is its lustre, scarcity, durability and so on. This intrinsic view corresponds to the

coherence definition of truth, with its emphasis on internal logical organisation. If one defines an analytic truth as one where its denial is a contradiction but it is ultimately itself a tautology, an equivalent expression of intrinsic value would go along the lines of: 'money works if we value it, and this is what makes gold good as money'.

2. **Fair value / correspondence theory of truth.** This suggests that we hold objects in comparison against an objective measure or scale of value of some sort, in the same way that the correspondence theory of truth suggests that a particular proposition displays a degree of congruity with reality. Value in this context is therefore construed as some sort of non-semantic object and is therefore a separate and discrete property of objects considered as valuable. It suggests that we value things because they possess a separate quality of value measurable independently of the object itself. That this value is often expressed in monetary terms perhaps reveals no more than the fact that money can be used both to reflect the current market price and some possible future imputed value.

Value is often expressed in this way for financial instruments and usually as part of an opinion about a particular fair value being true at a particular time. With respect to the stock market, for example, one cannot help but sense a slightly platonic undertone to year-end equity price targets ('In my ideal world, by December 31st I think this stock will be worth ...'). Each market analyst has an ideal (hence platonic) value for a particular company's share price, and our experienced reality has yet to reflect that. The tendency to think of value as a separate quality in this way most likely comes from a mental confusion between thinking of things in terms of their value as money on the one hand and transacting with them to produce a monetary balance (for the seller at least) on the other. Fair value is a subjective opinion of a particular economic agent, and it is only ever a coincidence that it is the same as the actual market price in any situation bar that of perfect (and therefore perpetual) equilibrium.

3. **Value in utility / utility theory of truth.** In the same way that certain propositions are considered true because they effect social cohesion or some equivalent general benefit, so we value what makes the individual or society happier or materially better off. From a collective point of view, things falling into this category might include education or healthcare, especially with respect to the latter in terms of the shared benefits of vaccination and the like (i.e., practices that are beneficial for the whole only if almost everyone participates). Because it is shared, utility has a particular local quality. In the UK and the US, tertiary education is seen as the key to personal financial success and also as a key driver for national economic growth. Countries such as Germany or Switzerland are still prosperous but with far fewer university or college graduates, in part due to different working and apprenticeship practices. There

are, of course, matters of utility that are universal and hold over time; subsistence (food) and shelter (housing) are the most obvious examples here. Little further needs to be said about utility from the perspective of the individual or the rational agent, as this concept provides the bedrock of classical economics in terms of the motivation for profit maximisation and as such has been discussed elsewhere.

4. **Value as a matter of popularity / truth as a popularly held opinion.** Certain things are held to be true simply because everyone thinks they are. An equivalence here might be the belief in the early modern period that astrology could predict the future or that the dot-com bubble of the late 1990s had redefined the business cycle so that aspects of profitability or going concern were no longer an issue for investors or company management, allowing share prices to rise to stratospheric levels. When considering stock market bubbles and the like, there are always a few Cassandras at the time but, generally, it is only when prices crash that the majority see the asset in question as having been overvalued. In this sense, a stock market crash is as popular an event as the prior run-up in stock prices, the main difference being that the rally reflects a growing belief in a bright future and the sell-off creeping doubt about it.

* * *

These four definitions are not exhaustive and could never be, since the process of valuation and the reattribution of value is an ongoing one. The search for definitions, in the manner of 'value is such-and-such', probably reveals more about how we think about the value of definitions than value itself. It may reflect some aspects of what value might mean, but without fully answering the question of what it is to value something. In a sense, fixing definitions is an exercise in meta-valuation. The problem might, however, lie in the question itself, in that we might be asking too much in terms of generality for such a question to yield a single answer that holds true always and everywhere. If generality of definition is a problem, then perhaps a more deflationary approach, while potentially yielding a less satisfactory answer, nonetheless leaves us on firmer ground with respect to what we actually do when we value things, thus providing, at the very least, a clearer limit to what we can clearly say about what value is.

In this way, we can say the following: something is valuable if, at a given time and in a certain place, we consider it so. Value only reveals its specific sense if it is localised, temporalised and socialised. That some things are considered valuable over extended periods of time or amongst diverse groups of people says less about the objects themselves than about desires and needs shared by the groups of people in question. Value acquires its meaning from the time and place of its occurrence. Based on our experiences from the past, we value things from a present with a view to the future. Where we lack experience, there is often a tendency to overvalue novelty until we gain experience about what the value of this new object or service really means to us.

As an alternative to money, the value of perishable goods (especially food) is generally measured in terms of 'shelf-life' or something equivalent. Supermarkets tend to discount goods as they approach the sell-by date after which they cannot legally be sold. In addition, many goods also have a 'use-by' date after the 'sell-by' date. Ultimately, food that has 'gone off' has no value as it is spoiled and cannot be eaten. This shows quite neatly how value is not always a monetary phenomenon; the consumption value of food survives its sell-by date (the limit of its monetary value to the retailer) in the form of its use-by date, after which it is deemed to have 'gone off' and is of little use to anyone except perhaps a composting enthusiast.

Unless circumstances are exceptional, food is generally not stored for the long term (say beyond the use-by date on certain canned or frozen goods), and if it is, this practice relates only to foodstuffs with extreme longevity or that are designed to be stored for the long-term and gain their value from the actual passage of time. Beverages like wine, which have to mature and can only really be drunk after a certain period of fermentation, illustrate this point. The producer of a particular good values his wares in monetary terms as production of that good is his means of employment, and he can only realise an income by selling it. While this means the consumer also has to value such goods in monetary form in order to purchase them, the value gained from comestibles would do as well to be measured in terms of health, wellbeing, longevity and the like as it would be in terms of money or even another numeric quantity such as calories. If one looks at the current obesity crisis, for example, there is clearly a qualitative issue with respect to the sort of food people eat that goes beyond the mere cost or calories being consumed.

With this approach, value is not defined as a property or a quality of a good or a service, nor is it something that itself has a fixed definition. Things are merely valuable if at a certain time we treat them as such. Valuation is an activity that is subjective and particular and things are only valuable in that context rather than having a separate property of being valuable. This may sound odd and perhaps a little underwhelming but, as a starting point for an analysis of economic activity, this approach to value differs from the classical ideal of homo economicus as a universal, rational figure standing outside time, bent only on maximising his own interest, whatever that might in fact be. This latter approach presupposes a fixed set of rules applying across time without variation. Explaining the excesses of a stock market bubble such as the US dotcom boom in the late 1990s is far easier if one drops rationality and the idea of maximising utility and instead looks at what people were actually saying at the time: that a new paradigm existed in the economy that justified stratospheric company valuations in terms of new metrics, such as 'price to clicks' on websites and suchlike. It may have been misguided in retrospect, but the dotcom boom provides an excellent insight into shareholder behaviour and the nature of valuation.

*   *   *

The attribution of value is the key activity in any economy and is itself social in context and dynamic in nature. In this way, while prices are historical facts and are thus the empirical evidence of value, the variations in price over time become the story of valuation for a particular group or community, or of society at large. What we value changes over time, and so value itself changes over time, but value carries its own history with it in terms of price. With this approach, economics becomes less of a search for fixed rules and more like an extended exercise in historical analysis.

Defining value in this way is not an attempt to marginalise macro-economic theory with respect to price theory or the relationship between supply and demand. It is certainly not an attempt to undermine the empirical framework of economics as a social science. It does, however, demand that economics be located in a historical, social, anthropological and cultural context in order for it to have meaning. For obvious reasons, science has a tendency to look for patterns, and this is most easily done through numbers. By widening our view of economics from a statistical examination focused on historical price-series to one involving the history of value as a particular and idiosyncratic activity located in time, the quantitative exercise of pattern-finding is significantly enhanced by the qualitative analysis of its social, political and cultural context.

As an example of this, we can look at long price-series for patterns, but, at the same time, ask questions about the way we value the object being priced differently through time. In this way, the true role of prices as a historical record of the attribution of value comes to the fore. For example, we could compare the value of gold in 1919 and 2019 in terms of its price in dollars. We could adjust this for inflation between the two dates, work out how the overall amount of gold that has been mined in the intervening period has added to the stock of gold and work out whether gold is cheap or expensive versus its own historical price series.

While there is nothing untoward with this activity, it over-looks how, until the suspension of the gold standard in 1914, gold had been treated as the bedrock of the international monetary system, and this memory loomed large in the thinking of the Great War's victors, notably the UK, with respect to a return to the normality of the gold standard and the *status quo ante bellum*. Much of the monetary history of the inter-war years is engendered by how there could not and ultimately would not be a return to the pre-1914 mone-tary world[12]. In 2019, aside from central bank reserves and a few notable industrial uses, gold was by and large treated as jewellery, not money (in the West at least). If there is a monetary crisis in the future, gold may once again be increas-ingly treated as money or as a foundation for a more stable monetary system in a far more direct way than it was in 2019. Indeed, while a return to the gold standard might be seen as part of a perfectly natural expression of the return to normality in 1919, such an opinion in 2019 would have engendered a severe critique of the entire monetary, fiscal, and political status quo and, as such, is would have been the sort of opinion held only by a small minority who, for this very reason, might be labelled as cranks. Whatever the price, the value of gold was different in 1919 than in 2019, especially with respect to our treatment of it as money as opposed to jewellery.

These days, gold has a number of medical uses as well as industrial applications relating to its high levels of conductivity. The remaining gold traded each year is done so for financial purposes by central banks and investors more generally. These investment purposes currently appear to fall well short of gold-as-money, at least by gold-standard criteria, since there is no official convertibility between national currencies and gold as there was pre-1914. As such, gold is often treated in the popular media as a slightly fringe investment – a pet rock[13]. Were more general questions over the public's faith in the money system to arise, gold and other precious metals might once again be more widely considered as suitable for the role of money and not just for the most part as jewellery. Gold would still be seen as valuable, but in a different way.

Whatever the proximate cause for the revaluation, if gold were to be more widely considered as a necessary type of money and not just as jewellery, the event would likely be recorded as a sharp rise in the price of gold in dollars or other currencies as people sought to own it as money. In the context of the idea presented earlier in the chapter of a hoarder being an untimely collector, the seemingly ahistorical calls of a small minority to turn back the monetary clock with a return to the gold standard might in time become a more mainstream position within economics, with gold bugs retroactively being seen to perform the role of prescient hoarders. The 'gold bug' eventually being right about the long-term price of precious metals is a useful example of the subjectivity of value. Being proven right about one's sense of value in this context is contingent upon the revaluation of gold from jewellery to money by a much wider spectrum of the population.

*   *   *

Another way of describing the relationship between price and value is to think of price in terms of an empirical exercise to establish *that* value has changed and a technical examination of *how* that change manifests itself over time. These are very much questions of the facts about a change in value and the means (the market) by which that change manifests itself. The question to what end or purpose the change has manifested itself is a separate one. This more amorphous question of *what* has changed with respect to value might better be located somewhere closer to the philosophical question of ethics, particularly concerning the concept of practical reason, the Aristotelian idea of the logical faculty of working out what to do in a particular situation. This essentially makes value into a type of feeling, one grounded in experience (whether personal or inherited culturally or socially) and expressed in the present but with an awareness of the future. This feeling of value, while it may be said to be real in an ethical sense, only becomes an empirical fact when market participants find it necessary or desirable to act economically by transacting.

The demarcation of price and value into the respective spheres of empirical knowledge and ethics is a key development for approaching the question of causality in economics. If one looks at an economic phenomenon such as inflation from a purely empirical perspective, there are a number of ways to examine the reasons for its occurrence. One can look at it from the point of view of demographics and a growing population: from the supply side of the economy (cost-push inflation relating to rising raw material costs for businesses); from the demand side (tax cuts or rising wages overstimulating demand relative to an economy's overall capacity); from an excess of private credit growth or monetary inflation driven by government or central bank policy, to name the key ones.

All of these are reasons that can be given to explain inflation as a purely empirical phenomenon, but none of them really address directly the question of why people behave differently. This is a question about the *feeling* that money is suddenly worth less and that it should be spent sooner, and this feeling about how one should behave is effectively an ethical question relating to value and not one lending itself to a purely empirical explanation that can be substantiated in terms of price or rational action relating to price.

It is widely believed, for example, that the lag between central bank policy changes (such as an interest rate cut) and their effect on the economy (higher borrowing, spending and potentially inflation after an interest rate cut) can be as long as a year to a year and a half. This concept of hysteresis (the delay between an event and its consequences) which suggests it takes a year or more for a rate cut to 'work its way through the economy' does have empirical grounds to work from, such as banks being slow to pass on the rate cuts to borrowers thereby delaying the inflationary credit impulse. The vagueness here might, however, also be an example of an impossible task that economics has set itself is in trying to address problems of an ethical nature (our feelings about value) by using the tools of scientific empiricism (i.e., price analysis). By confusing the boundary between the material (price) and the ethical (value), economics demeans its own, perfectly valid claims to the scientific by unwittingly allowing its empiricism to overstep the mark. This is particularly so given that inflation is, by its nature, a rate-of-change measure. When the issue of inflation reaches the front pages of the press, something is clearly changing in our collective value system, irrespective of the proximate event used to explain it.

In addition to the various material reasons cited earlier for the occurrence of inflation, there is also a suggestion of a psychological angle to the phenomenon in terms of inflation *expectations*. This view is driven by the idea that people's behaviour can be retuned by changes in the economy and that their behaviour today carries on into tomorrow as a result of this. When central bankers talk about inflation expectations becoming 'unanchored', they mean that higher prices today can cause consumers to expect higher prices on an ongoing basis, and this changes their wage expectations and consumption behaviour in a more permanent manner. This is what happens when inflation becomes 'sticky' (embedded) – the experience of the 1970s is a key example of this, particularly the spiral of higher prices and then higher wages to compensate for them.

Behaviour and psychology in economics are often treated as a different facet of the same question, particularly with respect to rational and irrational behaviour – the madness of crowds and so on. If, however, one draws a line between the material and ethical (between price and value), then when one is asking questions about economic behaviour with respect to value (and thus in the context of an ethical evaluation, not a price measurement), one is asking a different question in a different way, since the answer cannot be furnished in the same empirical way of conjecture and refutation that one might expect when examining and explaining a price series. By assessing inflation in terms of an ethical question about value, one is not necessarily looking for a tangible measurement as an answer. It may be comforting only to seek to quantify the degree to which goods and services cost more or that, correspondingly, money seems to be worth less; but in order to answer the question about a change in value, one needs to try to free oneself from any material bias.

If one looks at our economic value system as one of choosing between consuming and delaying consumption (saving) and thus as a system essentially grounded in time, then the change during a period of inflation is one of value, in which our collective time horizon shortens. The product of this change is rising prices, and this can be measured empirically as a rate-of-change function in terms of the consumer price index (CPI) or something equivalent. During periods of inflation, we tend to favour the present over the future, and thus consumption takes precedence over saving. In extreme cases of hyperinflation, life becomes a day-to-day struggle for survival in which all concern for the future disappears. Whether we actually acknowledge that money is worth less or whether we merely act in a way that is suggestive of it being so without really knowing (i.e., the rational vs irrational debate) is really of no consequence here.

There are a number of reasons that can be used to explain the manifestation of inflation in an empirical way, but the pervasive changes of habit during an inflationary episode in an economy are driven by a judgement about the relative value of time. The general change in prices remains the key measure of inflation in the economy, but it is our sense of time that has really changed with respect to our view of the world. Thus, the rate of change in inflation becomes a measure of how quickly our sense of time is itself changing.

One can thus both furnish a good explanation of why inflation is happening (our sense of time changing) as well as measuring it (via the rate of change in price levels) without always having to pin one's argument to a particular, favoured explanation of why inflation happens *in general*. The empirical explanation is likely to be not only complex and variegated but also contingent on the example in question and the experience of the individuals involved at that time. What will not be particular or idiosyncratic will be the cause of inflation – and that is a general foreshortening of the time horizon of economic agents, which can be measured as a general rise in the level of prices. Exactly the converse will be true of deflation as a general extension of the collective economic time horizon. Deflation could be characterised by the propensity to save rising relative to the propensity to consume (i.e., the delaying of consumption), with the result being a general fall in the level of prices.

*   *   *

Understanding the relationship between value and price helps to establish the type of question one can ask (and therefore answer) with respect to each, but it also allows us to reveal many of the more normative aspects of economics that are so conventional as to become rule-like. This becomes clear when applied to the scenarios that have been used to explain some of the key pillars of neoclassical economics such as utility. Some of these are contrived – for example, illustrating marginal utility by hypothesising what someone stuck in the desert would do if presented with a choice between a glass of water and a piece of gold. This is a variation on the classic diamond-water paradox, best illustrated by Adam Smith by contrasting the idea of *value in use* (water) with *value in exchange* (the diamond, as a proxy for money more generally). The paradox comes from the fact water is abundant, critical to life, but barely worth anything, while diamonds are largely without practical use but highly valuable. While Smith chose to suggest value derived from the cost involved in a good's production rather than its marginal utility to a particular individual (such as a glass of water to someone stuck in the desert), the real question at hand is the assumptions made in the very framing of the paradox itself.

The idea of a subjective theory of value, in which the value of something is derived from its use or attraction to a particular individual, explains how, in some situations, water can be more valuable than gold or diamonds. Yet the framing of the scenario reveals more about our tacit assumptions about the market than it does anything else. The paradox demands a context for meaning: water is always important, but sometimes gold (or diamonds or money more generally) is more so. If one is stuck on one's own in the desert, then there is no choice between water and gold. Without anything to spend the money (gold) on, and with no one around to trade with, the medium of exchange and convertibility (money) is irrelevant as there is no market.

In the example above, by making the choice between water (necessary for subsistence) and gold (as a form of money), one is really contrasting the pre-economic and economic state of being. A choice between water and gold in the desert is meaningless in economic terms since money (gold) is meaningless without a market. Markets and money are thus shown to be social in nature and the idea of rational individuals going *into* a market to maximise their utility is shown to be a false construct, as there can be no economics outside this forum of social interaction and no individual can stand outside the market and still be economic. Value appears subjective and contextual but meaningful economically only in a social context.

What this scenario of the choice between water and gold in the desert does illustrate quite neatly, though, is that the framework of our judgement about value is essentially one about time. As a matter of survival, consumption is always the first consideration. As soon as day-to-day survival is assured, the possibility emerges of saving some of what one could consume today for a later date. That is what the gold represents in this hypothetical scenario and, as such, it is doubly irrelevant – first, given the immediate need for consumption to survive (i.e., today is what matters not tomorrow) and, second, because money only has value in a social context provided by the plurality of the market.

If the scenario is modified such that the choice between water and gold is presented in the knowledge that there is a town with a market two days walk away, then the whole process of evaluation is changed. In this instance, with another question about time, can the individual survive two days of walking to get to the town to spend the gold on other consumable goods? Similarly, if the value of water is being considered in the context of its agricultural or industrial use (versus gold as money), then the nature of the question changes to one more reflective of an opportunity cost framed around a choice between investing more in production or just retaining (saving) capital, with water being treated as a commodity.

While the water-or-gold choice shows that we value utility, it cannot show that utility is the limit of that which we value. Because the scenario is one where the only concern is the situational immediacy of the now and there is no one with whom to create a market, the basic economic choice of consuming or saving is not present. For the castaway in the desert, the water is *invaluable*, as its consumption is a matter of survival.

The property of being invaluable cannot be expressed in numeric (monetary terms) for us to understand how important it is. While this shows on a trivial level that value need not always be expressed in monetary terms, it also illustrates how economic judgements only acquire significance within the economic sphere, and that sphere is a social one. Survival situations, those rendering consumption a necessity, allow no prospect of thoughts for the future and are therefore not economic. Consuming just to survive is one decision (if it can be called such); surviving with a view to the future is another.

If at one end of the scale we find survival situations that yield the term *invaluable* ('at no price'), at the other lies the term *priceless* ('at any price'). If one is looking for an example of that which is priceless, both as metaphor and object, something like 'the crown jewels' are a good starting point. Those stored in the Tower of London for example probably have some sort of nominal insurance value but, in modernity at least, they are not objects that would ever be sold or could ever be replaced; hence they are priceless. History suggests the ownership of such items often arises through conquest, pillage or theft – and thus that they are rarely items that are actually paid for. Clearly, the extreme scarcity value of some items puts them beyond the conventional means and context of valuation in purely money terms. What is important to note here is that, while no one can buy something that is priceless, in order that it be *considered* priceless is has to be considered as such by everyone.

* * *

When we say something is valuable, we sometimes feel there is a sense either that we imbue it with a certain quality or that we now recognise in it a quality previously latent. In both instances, value appears to have the character of an additional property of the object valued. If this is the case then, when I value something as worth £100, it is as if I say, 'I think object x is valuable *and* it is worth £100.' What we really mean, though, is slightly different: 'I think object x is valuable; it is worth £100.' In the latter case, the attribution of value is an event where the £100 means nothing without my valuation. An object cannot be valuable without at least one person thinking it so. Strictly speaking, it can only really have a monetary value (i.e., beyond the purely sentimental) if two people consider it valuable, as there is then the potential for a market to be made and that value realised in monetary terms through a transaction.

The tendency to think that the £100 value is a real (additional) property that can exist independently of one's valuation stems in part from a linguistic confusion. Money acts both as a system of account (a monetary amount something is worth) as well as a means of transaction (the number of pounds something cost when purchased). When there is a transaction, someone gets £100, and this is a real amount of money. Saying or thinking something is worth £100 is real insofar as it is an honest ethical judgement, but there is no corresponding empirical fact in terms of a transaction to show it to be so. Once a bargain is made, a price exists, which is an empirical fact *separate* to the individuals involved in its making. In this sense, price is objective. By contrast, value is subjective, as it still requires someone to hold the opinion that something is valuable and value thus cannot be impersonal because of this.

Part of the reason for this confusion about the value of things being a separate property independent of us comes from the way we use language to talk about value. Practical conventions in law and accounting, such as property valuation acting as the legal basis for a mortgage or the marking-to-market for listed securities (where the value of an asset on a balance sheet reflects the current market price of the instrument in question) make value seem 'real', even if the associated profits and losses are essentially 'unrealised' and exist only on paper. In legal and accounting terms, valuation is real. That we say things are valuable and that we give them a value is real but, ultimately, the empirical proof that value can be realised occurs when one monetises that value in a sale. A bank values a house being worth such-and-such a price because they are about to offer a mortgage on the property as a necessary part of a transaction that is about to happen. Even here, the bank's mortgage valuation is a judgement separate to the price generated in the trans-action, even if in this instance value and price are the same because the amount of the mortgage dictates the final transaction price.

There have been periods when value really did look to all intents of purposes to be objective. Neoclassical economics emphasis on a self-correcting market driven by (marginal) utility and the supply and demand of commodities can be seen as the product of an era (from the 1870s to 1914) where a highly stable monetary system (the classical gold standard) lent itself to this self-correcting view. This was an economic world where not only did utility play a central role, but price and value were effectively indistinguishable because of the obstacles to inflationary monetary debasement imposed by the gold standard. The danger here, of course, is in extrapolating from a status quo and making the assumption that those circumstances, particularly the monetary ones underpinning the economic system, are axioms of economics, not just temporary features of the current economic and monetary environment. For neoclassical economics, money could be portrayed as neutral and banks could be cast merely as intermediaries between borrowers and savers because that is what appeared to happen at the time. While the gold standard permitted Victorians to have a remarkably consistent sense of value, one that perhaps, because of its stability and longevity, had the appearance of being objective, historical coincidence falls far short of providing rules that hold through time.

Another example of a theory of value making sense within its own historical context is one relating to labour[14], and this is a particularly good example for understanding how we think of value based on experience and memory. It is ironic that if one sees the broad sweep of the industrial revolution as one characterised by a dramatic improvement in the harnessing of energy (initially through steam power) then the relevance of a (manual) labour theory of value was redundant even before it became the linchpin of Marxist thought[15]. The technological leap of the first industrial revolution dramatically increased productivity and therefore income, and with it the ratio of the saveable over the consumable, which in turn set up the conflict between labour and capital (or those who said they stood for them) on how this extra income should be distributed in monetary terms.

Clearly, many of our judgements about value come from our individual or collective experience. That a transition was occurring from manual work on the land to manual work in factories may well explain why labour was still used as a reference point in the nineteenth century for what 'work' meant, even though most of the extra 'work' that made all the difference was done by the coal and the steam – and this change was an exponential one, destabilising society and creating a host of new problems because of its very magnitude. Ultimately, the labour movement of the nineteenth century probably had more to do with the urbanisation of the masses and resulting class consciousness than the actual labour they performed, since the real revolution was one of energy, derived from the more productive use of fossil fuels.

In the same way a backward-looking labour theory of value lay at the heart of Marxist thought, so too did Malthus's *Essay on the Principle of Population*, through its use of positive and negative checks, describe a perfect picture of an equilibrium world of low population and GDP growth characterising more than a thousand years of economic experience[16]. Yet, even as Malthus wrote, technology was changing the quality of the soil and the efficiency with which it could be worked, and this, coupled with the other technological advances over the next 150 years, would see not only an explosion in the global population but a rise in the quality of living at the same time. Perhaps Malthus's mean-reversionary mind-set (increases in wealth and population would eventually be reversed due to pressures caused by dearth, famine, disease, war and so on) is again echoed in the stable-state modelling of modern neoclassical economics. That much of the world's population growth has come at a direct expense to the natural environment has sadly only been realised much more recently. Perhaps environmental degradation means there will be a reversion to the mean in our standard of living, only on a time scale too long for economists to model or of a nature too unpalatable for politicians to accommodate, especially if it occurs after a few centuries of pleasant growth.

★   ★   ★

A more contemporary example of potentially radical changes to our value system can be found in education, an undertaking not only personally invigorating and liberating but also contributing to progress in our collective knowledge as well as economic growth. While it is an endearing idea, attending university as something done for its own sake in the pursuit of knowledge is an increasingly rare phenomenon. For much of the last fifty years or more, a university or college education has meant that the life experience of the well-educated, white-collar worker has been one of ever-rising standards of living and opportunity. Service industries and the knowledge economy have flourished. Conversely, globalisation and technological progress (especially automation) has crushed the real wages of the blue-collar worker in the US and elsewhere in the developed world.

As the world economy became more integrated and global-ised, it became apparent that brains were essentially mobile but brawn was not. Education provided the gateway to the best service-industry jobs. One wonders whether the extraor-dinary value currently placed on higher education, witnessed by the enormous and ever-inflating fees required for college tuition, will still be the same in a few decades time when the true impact of digital disruption and artificial intelligence (AI) has made its effect felt in the professional playgrounds of the global elite. If digitalisation proves to be for services what globalisation and automation has been to goods, one wonders whether the real earning power of the average white-collar worker over the coming years will suffer the same fate as that borne by the blue-collar worker in the developed world since the 1970s. Not only would this likely be highly deflationary as AI muscles in on the white-collar world, we might also see a deflationary event in the value of college education, since the onerous cost of student debt that accompanies it would not be offset by a promise of higher future earnings.

*　　*　　*

What we value changes and the extent to which we value things is dynamic. The process is one that happens in the pres-ent but is based on our knowledge, collective and individual, of the past. Often the greatest changes and upsets occur when the present confronts us with a radically new reality for which we have few reference points. While valuation is always an active and subjective process, it can often be reactive in nature. Much of the time, our judgements about value do not need to change and only do so when jolted by some exogenous shock. It is often these shocks that reveal the true nature of our judgements about value since they can result in rapid and dramatic realignments of the economy and society. Behind all these judgements lies an understanding that all economic decisions ultimately relate to time, since they involve a choice between the present and the future, between consuming and saving. To understand more fully how thoughts of the future are the key to defining the economic sphere, it is necessary to integrate a theory of money and credit into a theory of value and price. This is the subject of the next chapter.

4.

THE MONEY VALUE OF TIME

The discussion of value in the previous chapter focused on what made things valuable rather than trying to define what value was in the abstract. What makes definitions attractive is that their strictness creates the veil of precision, and this precision allows us to infer a high degree certainty from which we can gain confidence. While this approach clearly has its psychological attractions, it also runs the risk of creating or demanding a sort of foundation myth to prove or justify the universality of the definition itself as well as the thesis behind it. Definitions, by their nature, have to hold over time, and everything must fit for them to hold. If it aspires to be a rule or an economic law, a definition held to be true now must always have been so and the back-story needs to be elaborated upon in order to be confirmatory. The commonly held definitions of money are no exception to this tendency. Laws do not tend to lend themselves to evolution or change.

In political philosophy, the idea of a social contract between rulers and the ruled grew in popularity during the Enlightenment. This process was in no small part due to Jean-Jacques Rousseau's 1762 work, *The Social Contract*, which conjured-up happy images of peasants sitting under trees in the Swiss town of Neuchâtel, exercising self-government and deciding together how they should be ruled. The idea of the social contract creating an equitable and rational basis from which the consent of the governed could be traced is still an intoxicating idea but it is just that: an idea, and one with few historical precedents, at least not in the sense that Rousseau envisaged. The social contract is in some ways an origin myth for a number of arguments underpinning representative government – it may make sense rationally or theoretically, but that's not how the story unfolded historically.

Likewise, if we start with a definition of money, and particularly one that makes sense now, there is a risk of starting to myth-make about the origins of money and what came before it. The experience of monetary history in the twentieth century (and beyond) teaches us that when a country's currency collapses, either an alternative type of money is used (often non-domestic, hard currencies like the US dollar) or the economy descends into a system of barter based on the idea of the 'communion of needs' – the good luck that the goods or services one person has to offer are actually wanted or needed by another person at that time, and vice-versa.

Money functions because of its convertibility and divisibility. Bank deposits can be converted to cash or spent via debit cards, and this spending converts money into goods or services. Money in the form of a domestic currency can also be converted to foreign goods or financial assets through the foreign-exchange markets. Since money can be used as a neutral medium of exchange, money societies overcome the problem of the communion of needs. Money facilitates trade, specialisation, investment, the honouring of contracts, technological advances and other factors contributing both to economic stability and progress. Yet, much in the same way that political philosophy has its hypothetical social contract, so the story of money takes the *post-monetary* description of barter and often assumes this to be exactly what happened *before* money as well. Because money as a medium of exchange is so much better than having to rely on the communion of needs, it often feels like money must have been invented to solve a problem. Markets can exist without money, but the network effect that money provides makes economic life after money hard to conceive as anything but a retrograde step.

The story of money might better be conceived as one of evolution to meet society's needs rather than of a one-off solution to a problem. The assumption that clever money replaced simple barter may not just be a question of bad history but possibly one of backward induction as well. Conversely, finding out 'the truth' about the historical origins of money does not necessarily create grounds from which to establish a fixed definition of what it is. This is particularly true when comparing complex and plural modern economies and societies with the ancient ones first using and writing about money. That would be to assume that once created, money hasn't changed or evolved or, at a more basic level, that once it appears, it exists in some way independently of its users and owners or that money's own history doesn't affect how we think about it now.

If asked for a definition, a clever economist might say money is the creation of the state and is ultimately used for the discharging of debt. This is the basic description of the state theory of money (or Chartalism), a nominalist view of money, which in its modern guise goes under the name of modern monetary theory or MMT[1]. If one were to ask a random passer-by to name something created by the state that is primarily used for discharging debt, one might be left waiting quite a while for this sort of 'correct' answer. The average person would probably describe money as what they got paid, what they pay for things with, what they save and, most likely, what they'd like more of. While the average person does use money to pay their taxes, describing money to them as a tool created primarily for discharging debts would likely get a shrug and a quizzical look. Clearly it is social, legal and contractual in some ways, but it always seems to be far more than that.

One way of illustrating the narrowness of this state theory of money is by comparing currency to certain 'official' documents also issued by states to their citizens. Saying money only exists to discharge debts (especially taxes) would be the equivalent of saying passports exist only to allow international travel or that driving licences only act as proof of being legally permitted to drive. These two documents are used in everyday life as proof of identity, permanent abode or even age if one is trying buy restricted substances such as alcohol or tobacco. It is clearly the mutually accepted use that matters, not the original, official purpose. While the legality of currency, passports and driving licences is synonymous with their validity and acceptance, this does not mean they can only be used for the purposes for which they were originally created.

Perhaps the right answer is that we are asking the wrong question. Money, as legal tender, may be the creation of the state and its purpose may be to discharge debts (in the form of taxes) but if I were to send my nephew and niece some cash in an envelope for Christmas, I am not really discharging a debt. To argue that this reflects some kind of social debt or obligation is tenuous at best; what I am doing is just using money as a gift, and this is how I would describe the action. So, if the strict *definition* of money is something that is a legal creation of the state used to discharge debts, when I use money as a gift am I using it *in the wrong way*? Clearly this is a nonsensical question.

The footballer George Best was once quoted as saying, 'I spent a lot of money on booze, birds and fast cars. The rest I squandered.' One can clearly spend one's money poorly (or well, depending on how one looks at things), but this is very different to spending money the wrong way. Ultimately one can do with one's money as one wills, so long as it is legal (and even legality is not necessarily a limiting factor). In a similar way to how value is a subjective judgement by the individual but one gaining economic meaning in the collective sphere of the market, so money can be used in myriad ways, but the ones that matter economically are those involving social (and therefore economic) interaction. The goal, then, is not to seek a strict definition of money but to ask a two-fold question reflecting the dynamic and social nature of markets: first, what are the jobs that we ask money to do; second, how well does a particular type of money or monetary medium do those jobs?

The standard text-book definition of money comprises a short list that generally includes its function as a system of account, as a means of payment and exchange and as a store of wealth or value. This may be a bit broader than the Chartalist definition but, nonetheless, this is how money is generally described if not defined.

It is generally true nowadays that a country has its own currency, which is treated as the legal tender there. Some countries use another country's currency if they have experienced a period of monetary instability (for example Zimbabwe using the US dollar after its hyperinflation in 2008) or back their currency by another country's in a currency board, where foreign currency reserves are held by the central bank to mirror the stock of domestic currency in circulation. The Eurozone shares the euro, and this is the legal tender amongst the different member states. There are historical examples of banks having the right to print their own notes, and this is still true in Scotland and Northern Ireland for example[2]. Showing that countries have and historically had their own currencies is different to saying that money replaced barter. It does, however, start to illustrate the point that the form money takes (in a particular country or at a particular time) and what jobs money generally does can in fact be quite different, even if the former heavily influences the latter, especially with respect to how well a particular type of money works.

Rather than looking at money as a system of account, means of payment and exchange and store of wealth in terms of a list of parallel definitions, we may in fact look at these functions as inherently linked. Money can do all these jobs (and more) simultaneously, and its functional status as money depends on how well it does them all at any given point. Money has been around for millennia, and the reason we describe it in a certain way has more to do with how we habitually use it than the actual form it takes. No longer limited to strict definition, we can simply look at money in terms of the jobs we ask it to do, how those jobs compare and contrast with one another and, from this, make a qualitative judgement about how well a particular country's currency (or more generally a monetary system – like the gold standard or fiat money) performs each and all of the jobs demanded of it.

The three principal jobs that money does are sufficiently pervasive and recurrent enough for us to recognise whatever fulfils them as money. Whatever the monetary medium (paper, metal, conch-shells, cigarettes to name a few), those using it must accept that it is money. Something must be accepted as money to be described as such, and the acceptance of money is always manifested by usage, as the usage shows that *this money* can do the jobs asked of it.

Some mediums are more universal than others – cigarettes for example rarely act as money outside prison – but this sort of example perhaps reveals that a given money has a social boundary, be it physical (in the case of a prison) or geographic (in the case of a nation's currency). Although physical and geographic boundaries are not a barrier in the digital age, crypto-currencies can still be called money if that is how people use them and therefore value them. Crypto-currencies are, however, neophytes to the monetary world; what remains to be seen is how well over time they perform the jobs to which we generally task money or whether these new types of money can take on new roles. Only then can we really say whether they are a *good* form of money.

What makes a particular type of money good? A key characteristic of good money is stability. A country's currency may be described as stable if it lacks volatility, either internally against a basket of goods (in terms of inflation) or externally against other currencies or both. This is especially true of a currency that does not continually depreciate externally against its peers, as depreciation is usually the sign of poor domestic fiscal and monetary policy, a poor balance of payments or an excess of debt (either in its own currency or foreign ones) relative to the productive capacity of the economy. The relationship between money and government (or central bank) policy is clearly a reflexive one with each affecting the possibilities of the other, but the measure of the relationship is still best made in terms of monetary stability or the lack of it. The idea of stability can be extended to money in general if one thinks of money as a single medium having to do several jobs at once, of which system of account, means of payment and exchange and store of wealth are just the most salient.

Stability comes from the faculty of a particular type of money to balance the various jobs we habitually ask money to do without one job or role dominating. This is particularly true of the influence of governments and central banks on the stability of a country's currency, with some types of money, especially commodity-based money, being better able to resist the generally inflationary predilection of spending by the executive, especially when financed by the central bank. If this is the criteria for judging a particular type of money as good or bad and valuing it as such, one can see how money's functional status and performative abilities are far more important than its strict definition. The scarcity of gold, for example, has historically made it adept as a store of wealth. The same scarcity (in this instance, of coin) also arguably makes gold a poor means of exchange and one that can also inhibit the necessary provision of credit or government spending. There are clearly tensions between the roles which money plays, and the stability of different monetary media over time reflects this through the phenomena of inflation and deflation.

In this way, the measure of money is a qualitative one about how well it does the jobs we assign to it, although this judgement is best quantified through the measurement of inflation and deflation. We can compare different types of money in terms of how well they perform rather than get stuck in a linguistic trap of defining what money is. If assessing the quality of a particular type of money is an exercise in assessing the balance between the jobs money does, one is necessarily admitting that there first must be tension inherent to any functional form of money itself. Because it has to do several jobs at once, money is both flexible but also essentially unstable.

★   ★   ★

The nature of money as a thing which has various roles to play but whose roles are often incongruent, if not outright contradictory, only really becomes clear if one admits the centrality of time to the economic decision-making process. The economic experience is essentially indexical. In economic terms, this means that economic activity has a point of view and that it acquires its significance from the context in which it happens. For economic value judgements, this indexicality is a temporal one. The economic agent decides and acts from his or her position in the *now* of the present, and this *now* stands in relation to the past and the future. These three tenses of past, present and future define the scope of the economic sphere. It is, therefore, no coincidence that these three tenses are integral to the jobs we most frequently ask money to do. Money has *tenses* because the jobs it does are tensed, and this is the source both of money's ubiquity but also of its inherent instability.

As a system of account, money sits in the past tense. As a means of exchange and payment, it sits in the present tense. As a store of wealth, it looks forward to the future. Because the economic experience occurs in the present with a knowledge of the past and awareness or view to the future, so must money, as a single medium, perform all its temporal roles simultaneously in order to function as and be valued as money. This is what we want and need money to do. The history of money suggests that when money fails at one of its key temporal jobs, it eventually fails at all of them. In a hyperinflation, money ceases to function as a store of wealth and this ultimately leads to its failure as a means of exchange. In a period of extreme deflation, issues relating to bad debt, insolvency, unemployment and collapsing consumption show money failing as a means of exchange and payment. That this can result in the collapse of the banking system ultimately means extreme deflation can result in money ceasing to be store of wealth even though deflation is 'supposed' to make the spending power of money increase over time.

These temporal roles that money plays not only dominate the others, but they seek to dominate each other. As a means of exchange and payment, money facilitates consumption beyond the mere communion of needs, and this role ought to be considered inherently inflationary. As a store of wealth, money facilitates the delaying of consumption to the future, and thus ought to be thought of as inherently deflationary. It is the interrelationship of money as a means of exchange and payment on the one hand and as a store of wealth on the other that provides the fulcrum for understanding inflation and deflation in an economy, as this reflects the balance of aggregate economic decision-making oscillating between the present and the future: consume now or save for later.

Money as a system of account looks backwards, recording the history of valuation in the form of prices. The process of accounting is essentially relational in the sense that historical snapshots are compared to one another and this focuses on memory and experience, with all the individual and collective cultural and social influences entailed. Systems of account require stability in order to function and the more neutral any given monetary system is with respect to inflation or deflation, the more continuous and meaningful the process of accounting and valuation can be.

Money's ability to act as a system of account is not only compromised by the more dramatic types of monetary debasement and hyperinflation, but also by the more insidious drip-drip of low but persistent levels of inflation. The latter perhaps reveals a sort of threshold to our sense of economic value judgements, where sufficiently imperceptible changes might not catch our attention on a day-to-day basis but that, over time, mean our points of reference turn out to be dramatically altered. The effect of low but persistent inflation on money is like looking up when swimming in tidal waters only to find one has drifted dramatically from where one started out or thought one was heading. Given the centrality of valuation in the economic decision-making process and since valuation is ultimately a matter of knowledge and experience, the quality of stability in any monetary system is thus paramount, as it provides a sense of continuity between the past and the present.

Money as a means of exchange and payment exists in the present tense and is the realm of consumption and spending as well that of discharging previously incurred obligations such as taxes and other debts. As mentioned previously, Chartalism describes money as a creation of the state, which exists for the payment of taxes, but the difference between this and money's role as a means of payment and exchange can be illustrated most clearly by the advent of crypto-currencies such as bitcoin. Because of block-chain technology, cryptos are decentralised and therefore are not so much supra-national (like the euro in the Eurozone), multi-national (like the US dollar in its capacity as the de facto global reserve currency and the common choice for currency boards), international (like gold in the gold-standard era) but non-national. Despite not being the currency of any country, bitcoin can be used to pay for goods and services or for discharging debt. In this sense, it is fulfilling one of the jobs we generally require of money while existing in an intentionally decentralised form on the blockchain. So long as it functions (or is allowed to function) as a means of payment or exchange, bitcoin exists to negate the state theory of money.

Bitcoin, new as it is, has yet to prove itself as a *good* form of money. It is notoriously volatile, and as such has yet to qualify as a sound system of account (from the perspective of the stability needed to convey our sense of value from the past to the present). Logically speaking, bitcoin ought to be an excellent system of account as its structure makes the supply finite and this precludes the sort of monetary inflation that can wreck our sense of value in terms of continuity with the past. The finite stock of bitcoin certainly makes it a logically perfect store of wealth, though whether having a fixed stock of base money is compatible with long-term economic or demographic expansion is another question altogether.

Yet the stability argument, however strong it is, only holds internally. Bitcoin is non-national and decentralised and, like gold in the era of floating currencies, it is priced in national currencies, and so long as nation-states and their currencies continue to exist, the 'floating' relationship between bitcoin and national currencies will be a source of volatility. Short of its universal adoption as a world currency, decentralised crypto-currencies such as bitcoin will always suffer from the perpetual issue of geopolitical competition and conflict manifesting itself in the ebb and flow of nations' currencies due to domestic monetary and fiscal policy, foreign policy and the balance of payments and international flows of capital that derive from them.

If its status as a neophyte on the monetary scene means it has yet to prove decisively whether it really is a good form of money, bitcoin nonetheless is a superb illustration of the point that if something does the jobs we require money to do, we can treat it as money, even if the form is new and therefore essentially untested and unproven. Something becomes money when we start *using* it in the way we normally use money. Whether we *call* something money is just a matter of casuistry. High-handed pronouncements about whether something (such as bitcoin) is or is not money are essentially meaningless if one's criteria for something being money is a matter of it being used as such.

Finally, money as a store of wealth necessarily occupies the future tense, since saving money is the act of delaying consumption. The idea of saving did not start with settled society but its characteristics as a human trait become more apparent when hunter-gathering gave way to agriculture. Even the subsistence farmer must save seed-corn for the next planting or suffer the knowledge that starvation beckons. The very act of farming implies planning, and the emergence of settled, agricultural communities forms a key step in the development of the economic sphere as we now recognise it, particularly with respect to the appearance of credit and money. Central to this process is man's awareness of himself in economic time with respect to his memory and experience of the past, his needs in the present and how his prospects for the future depend on his actions in the present, especially the balance of consumption against saving. The gradual emergence of money subsequent to the first settled communities reflects its existence in a social milieu involving nascent concepts of duty, mutual obligation and right[3].

Because economic decision-making is an activity that takes place in time, for money to function it must simultaneously reflect links to the past, the demands of the present and the possibilities of the future. Since money has to be functional to be useful, the pressures put on money with respect to consumption (which tends towards the inflationary) are always competing with the awareness of the need to save (a process delaying consumption and tending towards deflation). In the shifting balance between consumption and saving, competing pressures appear in the economy through money in the form of inflation or deflation. In addition to this, to be an effective system of account, money has to be stable in order that comparisons of prices in the past remain relatable over an extended period of time, and this stability has to derive from the degree of balance between the inherently contradictory inflationary and deflationary forces that exist in money in terms of its role as means of exchange and as a store of wealth. Money, and those who use it, exist in a reflexive relationship between consumption and saving.

★ ★ ★

There is a fourth temporal role that money plays, just as critical but tending to be less frequently discussed, and this is not just because it has a French name. The idea of *numeraire* relates to money performing the role of an abstract and fixed measure of value. This demands that it is a constant and therefore makes it an expression of the perpetual or timeless. This is different to money's role as a system of account, since the latter relates to the job of comparing historic prices to one another. The previous chapter discussed the demarcation of price and value, and numeraire relates specifically to the idea of value as expressed in monetary terms.

What money as numeraire and money as a system of account have in common is the functional need for stability, and this need is far greater with respect to numeraire since, while prices can be indexed-linked (to inflation), the idea of value or values, with their ethical connotations, cannot be adjusted in the same way without becoming fundamentally meaningless. This is the sense of the phrase 'lacking a moral compass', and it applies equally to our sense of value (economic and otherwise) during periods of extreme monetary and economic instability. Such periods usually coincide with social and political convulsions in which the moral framework of a society can be put under immense pressure. Because our sense of economic value is tied to the same ethical framework that operates outside the economic sphere, it should come as no surprise that the former can become unhinged during periods of social unrest. Criminality and lawlessness become rife in periods of economic dislocation, which themselves are often characterised by extremes of deflation or inflation.

The functional success of money as numeraire can be illustrated by a comparison between the nineteenth century and the current era. If one looks at the literature of the 1800s with an eye to discerning how people thought of money, one can see that the tendency to describe social status in terms of monetary income on a per annum basis reflects this sense that money had a fixed value[4]. A contemporary reader of fiction presented with the character of a gentleman with an income of £500 per year would know immediately what that meant, not only in terms of lifestyle but also in terms of social status, and this would likely be as true if one was talking about the year 1800 as it would the year 1850 or 1890.

In the more inflationary era in which we live, wealth has tended to be viewed in terms of the monetary value of possessions such as houses, share portfolios and the like rather than money itself as expressed as an annual income for example. This is the case because inflation makes the idea of money as numeraire a more tenuous proposition. In the ultra-financialised world of the twenty-first century, even the possession of goods no longer denotes wealth in the same way it did even fifty years ago. A new car, the purchase of which used to mean that 'someone was doing well', is now more likely to be leased than bought for cash, and it is the pervasive use of credit that tends to sever the link between goods and the meaning of their monetary value. At its heart, this reflects the erosion of the idea of money as a fixed measure of value, which in turn transforms the value of ownership (as opposed to mere possession or occupation) itself. This perhaps explains why there is now a tendency to look at intangibles such as lifestyle (education, fitness, diet, attitudes and so on) as a new measure of wealth rather than just the possessions someone has.

That money could function well as numeraire in the nineteenth century can be explained in no small part by the fact that this was the era of commodity-based money, which culminated in the classical gold standard. That gold is itself inert and scarce makes it ideal for the role of a perpetual and unchanging benchmark against which to value things in monetary terms. This of course stands in contrast to the historically inflationary tendencies of fiat money. The extended discussion of value and the expression of value in monetary terms in the previous chapter suggests that, while we are still in the habit of treating money as numeraire ('my house is worth £1,000,000' and so on), commodity money *does this job better* than fiat money. By contrast, the tendency of fiat-currency regimes to be inflationary suggests that they are better at performing the monetary function of exchange and payment. This is particularly true if one adheres to the temporal schema that exchange and payment are a matter of consumption and exist in the present, and this gives them an inherently inflationary bias.

If one thinks of valuation as a type of ethical decision, one can see how adherence to the gold standard allowed money to function well as a fixed measure of value as it was in some ways a matter of belief. The gold-standard era saw the championing of a particular view of money where a currency had an intrinsic value that needed protecting, especially from the tendency of governments to subvert its value through debasement. Never fully universal, the gold standard should probably be considered more of an institution with members than a universal world currency.

If the gold standard were a religion, it would be Roman Catholic to fiat money's Protestantism. Not only did it require uniformity of belief, but also strict observance in that governments, banks and private corporations had to *act out* the fiscal and monetary disciplines dictating the correct responses to the catechism of the flow of bullion between countries from trade, and this in turn reflected the supply and demand fluctuations displayed in domestic prices. One could say this is a bit like the Roman church demanding attendance every Sunday as opposed, for example, to the tendency in the Church of England in the eighteenth century to permit 'occasional conformity' in which attendance at the feasts of obligation (Christmas and Easter) was enough to prove one's faith. For governments using fiat currency, a balanced budget is a choice, not the article of faith it had largely been during the classical gold standard era.

The gold standard could only continue to function if all the rules were followed all the time, and gold itself became a sort of international institution of veneration not dissimilar to the orthodoxy of the Catholic church during the Middle Ages, with all the attendant conflicts with national rulers and their domestic political needs. The difficulty in readopting the gold standard following the capital destruction and profound indebtedness caused by the First World War perhaps suggests that turning back the clock to the *status quo ante bellum* was, like lapsed faith, possible only in the knowledge that one's faith has lapsed and may do so again.

The idea of money acting as an abstract standard of value or numeraire is therefore perhaps at best an ideal, or at least one whose existence in a truly functional form is coincident with the passing reality of a particular monetary system for a given period of time. A commodity-based international monetary system whose bullion flows limited the credit cycle and with it inflation, a generally limited form of government (outside wartime) and serendipitous discoveries of gold in California, Alaska, Australia, South Africa and elsewhere (to offset the deflationary effect of gold's inherent scarcity amidst a growing global population), all acted in concert to create an arguably unique period of monetary stability in the nineteenth century where, by happenstance, money could be treated as a fixed measure of value even to the backdrop of the boom-bust economic cycle that became more apparent with industrialisation.

★   ★   ★

Money will always struggle to perform the truly abstract, atemporal role of a benchmark of value at the same time as it has to act as a store of wealth and a means of exchange, the interrelation of which marks a constant flux between the present and the future. In order to be functional, money has necessarily to fall short of perfection with respect to any one of its various jobs. The study of money thus becomes the study of the balance of imperfections in the roles it performs. One of the consequences of the apparent stability of metallic or commodity money, and particularly the limited control over it that governments had (in contrast to money in the fiat era), is that money appeared neutral with respect to understanding economic interactions and, as a consequence, money and private credit creation (especially through the banking system) was an awkward addendum for much of classical economics. As a result, the importance of credit creation and therefore of who performs this role (whether it be banks or governments via fiscal deficits) is still in some circles somewhat of an open question, especially with respect to the debate about whether banks create credit or merely act as intermediaries between savers and lenders.

While the value of money is measured in terms of inflation and deflation, amounts of money are measured in numbers through counting. That we use one medium to do all the several jobs money has to perform is both its strength but also a source of confusion about how it works. It is likely that any practical attempt to deconstruct money into its component parts would mark the point at which it ceased to function as money. At the same time, it is unclear whether it is possible to construct a logically perfect form of money due to the inherent conflicts between the roles money usually performs.

One could, for example, consider the foreign-exchange assets known as special drawing rights (SDR's) at the International

Monetary Fund as an ideal store of wealth (for governments at least), but they fall short of really being money or even a form of currency because, by their very nature, they are not readily usable as a means of exchange or payment, at least not by the man in the street[5]. SDRs, therefore, suffer exactly the same problem with relation to money as a universal language such as Esperanto suffered with respect to natural language. While by no means logically perfect, Esperanto's very claim to universality was also its fatal weakness, as no one actually owned it culturally or historically. It is in the character of money to fulfil several potentially contradictory roles simultaneously, but it is this very mutability that makes it a functional tool that is rarely discarded once adopted. In this sense, a logically perfect language could be seen as analogous to a world currency; reality falls far short of the ideal.

There are of course practical problems too – the relationship between domestic economic concerns and those of a more international nature are another facet of this. The history of the US dollar in the twentieth century is a prime example. When the US is in trouble, it tends to favour its domestic economy rather than its international obligations. This was true in 1933 during the great depression and again in 1971 when the country was mired in economic stagnation and war. On both occasions, the US defaulted and devalued the dollar against gold.

Sometimes the money system itself is the problem. The Bretton Woods settlement in 1944 linked the dollar to gold, but in order for other countries to get access to dollars (for trade and central-bank reserves), the US needed to run a current-account deficit to allow dollars to flow out of the country. In the long term, this meant more dollars, and this weakened the dollar's standing against gold over the ensuing decades. The consequence of this so-called Triffin dilemma was a conflict between the domestic role of the dollar in the US economy and its status as an international reserve asset linked to gold at a fixed price. The negative balance of payments that the US had to run to allow the dollar to function as the currency of international trade and reserves led to a gradual outflow of bullion, resulting ultimately in the convertibility of the dollar for gold being suspended[6].

*   *   *

To summarise: money does a number of jobs. The dominant ones are temporal and reflect our day-to-day economic experience as one being based in the present, where the past resonates but where the prospects of the future are always on our minds. Is this really an original proposition? One push-back against the argument that suddenly looking at money as a mirror of our economic imperatives with respect to past, present, and future is somehow a novel observation would be to point out that we all already have the concept of the time value of money.

The yield curve, representing the structure of interest rates over time, already shows that money has different costs at different maturities, and thus the cost of money in terms of time is nothing new. This is of course true, but one has to distinguish between interest rates as a measure of the cost of borrowing and money as a store of wealth itself. This is the difference between looking at time in terms of money (the cost of credit) and money in terms of time (a store of wealth).

The difference between time in terms of money and money in terms of time can be illustrated by contrasting two forms of 'saving'. First, one puts some cash in a biscuit tin and keeps it under the bed. Here, money just acts as a store of wealth, in the sense one can use it for consumption at some point in the future, so long as the bank notes or coins remain legal tender, but the amount of money does not change as no interest is earned. When one 'saves' by depositing money in a bank, one is definitely still saving (from a personal perspective of delaying consumption) but one is simultaneously lending to the bank in return for interest, and this means depositors are creditors to the bank as well as being savers.

This lending is not an additional act to saving. By depositing one's savings in a bank, the saver is merely *investing* in the sense of choosing the manner in which they save. The idea of investing is perhaps clearer if one thinks back to the age when money took metallic form. One could save by holding specie (gold and silver) outside the banking and financial system, but in order to earn interest, one had to deposit and lend. The logic of this is born out in the famous saying attributed to James Pierpont Morgan that 'gold is money and everything else is credit'. What this means is that monetary gold and silver are unique in that their physical possession involves no contingent liabilities of the sort normally born by a credit agreement. The biscuit tin full of cash is a kind of diminutive modern equivalent to the hoard of gold, and both are really just extremely conservative forms of saving, with the possession of cash acting as protection against a bank run or something similar. The sense of this type of cautious saving comes from how we talk about *holding* cash rather than *investing in* cash.

When one is talking in general about storing wealth as one of the jobs money does, one is thinking about the money value of time measured in terms of inflation and deflation. When one is talking about credit, one is thinking about the time value of money in terms of the cost of interest at any given maturity. The fact that the nominal (headline) interest rate one receives by lending consists of a 'real' rate and an inflation component belies the simultaneity of lending and saving in the act of making a bank deposit (or lending more generally). In this way, lenders are subject both to the time value of money (the real interest rate) and the money value of time (through inflation or deflation), both of which can either be positive or negative depending on the wider circumstances in the economy, monetary policy and so on. Therefore, the nominal interest rate reflects the real interest rate creditors receive, adjusted for the money value of time in terms of inflation or deflation at any given moment.

★   ★   ★

When one starts to talk about credit and money, there is a danger of getting stuck into another genesis debate of the sort discussed earlier over whether money really did emerge as a 'cure' for the barter economy[7]. Ahistorical or not, when the question of the origin story of credit takes place in the context of money, one often ends up with a theoretical question as follows: was the first bit of money deposited in a bank to allow the bank to make a loan to someone else, or did the bank actually create the money in the form of a deposit without first needing any money to do so? This is of course really the question of whether banks are intermediaries between savers and borrowers on the one hand, or credit-creating (and therefore money-creating) institutions on the other.

Questions of credit involve obligations in the future, and these presume social relations but not necessarily of a monetary form. Even if it falls short of an actual social contract, a government's ability (if not right) to tax in a settled community has to involve some kind of common benefit or idea of a common good, even if it is just the periodic guaranteeing of the safety of that community from external threat. That these taxes were paid in kind or in coin is in a sense secondary to the idea of an obligation to pay underpinning them, even if that obligation was sometimes enforced rather than being a matter of consent. The point here is that the form money takes (coin, paper, or something else) is not relevant to the idea of the provision of credit, since the latter is a matter of the social relations of temporal obligation of a similar sort to the obligation to pay tax.

The confusion about credit comes from lending in money form, specifically the characteristics of money as a thing doing several jobs at once. If one starts with a choice between consuming and saving, anything one has in excess of subsistence is something one could save. In the somewhat contrived scenario of a subsistence farmer, seed-corn or the equivalent is saved for the next planting. If that farmer is particularly successful and the harvest particularly bountiful, he or she might have more than is needed for subsistence and replanting. This can either be exchanged for something else (including money), saved (although agricultural commodities perish over time so this isn't a viable long-term option) or *lent* to someone else. One can lend for interest, and this basically means getting back more than one lent as the price of lending. Interest need not be monetary interest, but it is always a cost based on time.

What is necessarily true of this somewhat crude agricultural example is that, when it comes to lending physical commodities, one can never lend more than one has. Even short positions in the commodity futures markets require physical delivery unless the short position is 'rolled' to a more distant delivery date when a particular futures contract matures. When one is lending money, however, this restriction does not occur and one can ultimately lend as much as one wants to, even if, in reality, lending is limited by considerations of prudence relating to the borrower's creditworthiness. A technically unlimited lendability is a property of money separate from the idea of lending and credit, and this can be shown by contrasting the way money and the physical commodities are lent.

It is the properties of money itself that permit the action of borrowing and lending to be a simultaneous act of consumption of credit in the present (by the borrower) and an act of investment for the future (by the lender) that can permit the lender to apply leverage, or lending more than they have. What makes money special is that it acts as a means of exchange and payment and as a store of wealth *at the same time*. It can do jobs for the present (consumption) and the future (saving) simultaneously, and this means it can be lent with leverage and thus, through the provision of credit, one is essentially lending time (the idea of drawing future consumption into the present through contingent monetary debt obligations).

Money *is* time, not the other way around. The formation of any community or society implies some social ties and obligations, and some of these obligations relating to the legal or contractual obligations of tax or debt can be binding over time. But when it comes to saving and lending in a pre-monetary society, one cannot lend more than one has in terms of physical commodities. This is a restriction that money does not have. Monetary credit is in essence the creation of borrowed time, which itself reflects the temporal jobs money has to do for it to be useful. Because this means that money has the propensity to be lent with leverage, one can say that banks act as money-creating institutions.

Saving is the act of delaying consumption to the future and lending is the act of offering those savings out to someone else, and this can only happen if there is someone who wants or needs to borrow. Borrowing is therefore concerned with drawing some of one's consumption from the future into the present. How this borrowed money is used is a question of the circumstances specific to the borrower, and this can be explained in terms of the borrower's own time horizon. An example of *bad* borrowing would be putting one's weekly shopping on a credit card and running up debt as a result, even if this meant the short-term necessities of subsistence were met. An example of *good* borrowing might be a company borrowing to build a factory or an individual taking on debt to pay for a university education. These are both acts undertaken in the present with a view to the future, and this is true even if the borrowing results in an act of consumption in the present (such as the purchase of materials needed for that new factory). Borrowing for consumption is thus an act of dissaving, while borrowing to invest for the future is effectively leveraged saving. That one can look at actions resulting from borrowing as being good and bad is again a reflection of the idea of the 'for what' in our economic value system being essentially an ethical judgement.

The type of borrowing involving consumption differs from the sort relating to investment. The former is clearly motivated by the needs or desires of the present, while the latter looks to the future. If one's measure of economic health is growth (or at least stability), then the short-termism of borrowing for consumption has to be contrasted with the more far-sighted aspects of borrowing for investment. Real interest rates (headline interest rates less inflation), as a reflection of the real cost of borrowing, reflect the degree of confidence in the future. Higher real rates suggest a strong demand for credit because of an optimistic view about future levels of growth or confidence that good times will last. It is the lasting of the good times that matters here – real rates rise because savers demand a higher rate of return in the context of the pressure to consume over the need to save for the future. Real rates tend to be lower when there is less demand for credit or when credit conditions are tight – the latter is often a situation arising when lenders perceive that borrowers are overindebted and when consumption is falling as a result. Economic expansions are characterised by growing confidence and a lengthening time horizon, and vice-versa during downturns and recessions.

The expansion and decline of the collective investment horizon in an economy can best be observed through a close monitoring of the credit cycle, both quantitatively but also with respect to qualitative considerations of capital projects, research and the like. The expansion of private-sector credit, closely linked to a growth in GDP, is almost by definition an expression of rising economic confidence in the future. Within particular sectors of the economy, rising borrowing to fund investment is usually described as the capital expenditure (or capex) cycle, and this reflects a rising degree of corporate confidence in higher profits in the future. The fact it is a cycle belies the imperfections of capitalism in terms of over-investment and rising competition eroding the supra-normal profits of individual companies through time, and eventually the cycle turns and, with it, the investment horizon starts to foreshorten.

The shortening of the collective economic horizon prior to a recession can be seen by the common pre-recessionary indicator of the inversion of the interest-rate yield curve, where its normally upward-sloping shape (reflecting a higher interest cost of borrowing for a longer duration) changes so that short-term interest rates are higher than longer-dated ones.

Banks generally borrow in short-dated instruments (using deposits, commercial paper or wholesale markets) and lend for longer durations, but an inverted yield curve makes this unprofitable. Lending standards tighten, the provision of credit falls and, more often than not, recession follows. Recessions are usually characterised by companies selling-off assets, sacking workers, paying down debt and raising equity, all in the pursuit of the goal of balance-sheet repair. For companies, reducing balance-sheet risk through debt-deleveraging is the consummate act of the reduction of the investment time horizon. When enough demand has been destroyed and supply has left the market, the bottom of a recession marks the shortest point in our collective time horizon and the cycle can start again.

More generally, money, credit and time are bound together by interest, and particularly the compounding of interest over time. The time value of money is measured as an interest rate, and that interest, expressed numerically as the price of money, makes debt compound through time. This is the key reflexive relationship within the temporal economics of money. That the compounding of interest is not a linear function but rather an exponential one over time is really what makes money matter in relation to credit and interest. The non-linear process of compounding is what makes lending worth it and debt a burden.

It is not just the charging of interest but the manner in which interest compounds over time that allows us to enjoy a monetary profit from the delayed gratification of saving, and this is what underpins the voluntary decision to delay consumption to the future. The financialisation of the global economy in many ways reflects the increasing monetisation of time and the inherent complexity that causes. Because the act of saving is always in competition with the act of consuming, rising economic confidence during periods of economic expansion, when it feels like tomorrow will be like today forever, puts pressure on the tendency to save and thus those who want to lend their savings demand more, hence rising real interest rates. In a recession, where confidence is low and consumption is subdued, this pressure on savers abates and real interest rates fall. An analogous situation occurs in an economy where the consumer is over-indebted. The act of servicing debt weighs on consumption and real rates tend to fall. Lending becomes riskier in these circumstances and credit conditions are described as 'tight'.

While time seems to pass in a linear fashion, day by day, the relative value of credit (from the point of view of borrower and lender) progresses in a non-linear fashion due to the way interest compounds over time. In theoretical terms, this is where we have to abandon Newton's idea of time as a fixed system of measurement in favour of Einstein's concept of the passage of time being relative to the bodies concerned. The result is that the temporal perspectives of economic agents are subject to constant change, and this renders the relationships between people and institutions within the economic sphere (in terms of creditor and debtor, rich and poor and so on) not only dynamic, but relational and ultimately indexical (in the sense that they can only be understood from a particular economic agent's perspective). This has been true from the earliest money societies in the fertile crescent of Meso-potamia and is still as true today. Rather than being an eighth wonder of the world, the compounding effect of interest over time, at least in money societies, is a – if not *the* – principal vector of relative inequality within society[8].

The divisive effect of compound interest on social equality lies at the core of Thomas Piketty's thesis in *Capital in the Twenty-First Century*. A long and vigorous period of economic growth in France between the end of the Franco-Prussian War and the First World War had led to the emergence of wide-spread inequalities of wealth. During this period, the owners of capital merely benefited from their wealth compounding at an increasingly faster rate than the rate at which the econ-omy was growing. Time was not passing equally for labour and capital.

The intractability of the problems compounding causes in the balance between rich and poor is illustrated when Piketty describes the period of 1914–1945 in France as being an example of the 'compression of inequality'[9]. It is usually the poor who suffer most from economic dislocation – both from inflation, which affects those who spend most of their income on food and energy, and deflation, during which job losses from falling demand often affect unskilled and semi-skilled labour the most. To highlight a period of two world wars, a depression and Nazi occupation as a 'win' for equality, especially in the light of France's enormous sacrifice of life in the Great War (during which poor males made up the bulk of the soldiery), shows not only the depth of the problem but also the iron grip that the non-linear progression of time has on the economy. To do Piketty justice, he goes on to add that this compression in equality was 'in no way harmonious or spontaneous'[10]. Perhaps this is an economist's way of describing the tragedy of the twentieth century, but it nonetheless reveals the extent of the task of those whose stated aim is truly to increase social equality.

*   *   *

If there is such a thing as economic time, then it clearly does not pass equally for borrowers and lenders, and this is purely due to the effect of how interest compounds over time. Notwithstanding events relating to bad debt, default or restructuring (or debt jubilees in which debts are periodically written-off), since interest is always compounding, for there to be saving there has to be more lending and, for that, there has to be more borrowing and spending. As a non-linear function, compound interest might therefore best be treated as an exogenous influence or force on the social cohesion of a given country or community, and managing the consequences of this is one of the main preoccupations of politics. An overindebted economy becomes like a monocrop culture but one whose sole output (more money from the accrual of interest, which is in turn lent out in the form of more debt) effectively sows itself through the process of compounding. For the debtor at least, accrual is certainly an unusual punishment, as the sentence becomes more onerous as time passes.

If real interest rates are a measure of time in monetary terms, then lower rates usually follow a period of monetary tightness and point to low growth, and higher rates the opposite. If one thinks of this in terms of a moving time horizon, low rates represent a shortening time horizon and a collective decision to reduce consumption and investment while higher rates suggest a lengthening one, characterised not only by an urge to consume but also a sense in which that urge to consume will continue. Consumption here refers to resources in general, not just subsistence, and the idea of credit (lending one's savings to others for them to spend now or the leveraging of capital by banks to effect the same outcome) is implicit in this – companies invest in capital projects because they are optimistic about the future in the present not because they know what the future holds. That lending occurs within the context of the compounding effect of interest through time, and this process itself adversely affects the propensity of debtors to consume due to the build-up of debt service costs, is to define the credit cycle. The interest rate being considered here is the real rate, not the nominal (or headline) rate. Low or even negative real rates occur during periods of low real economic growth or during periods of capital destruction.

What of headline or nominal interest rates, which combine real rates with a market estimate of inflation? While it is generally observed that periods of inflation are characterised either by high energy prices, rising wages or both, periods of economic growth do not necessarily have to be inflationary, even when consumption is rising (hence the higher energy prices and rising wages). Rapidly growing economies with rising standards of living for the many usually experience high real interest rates, as demand for consumption creates a premium for saving (delaying consumption). Periods of high debt, falling consumption, falling real wages, falling investment and low growth see money being used primarily as a store of wealth and are deflationary. Rising consumption and investment, reflected in a sharp growth in the money supply due to a strong demand for credit in the public and/ or the private sector, can take an economy beyond its productive capacity and this is when inflation starts. This is when money's role as a means of exchange and payment starts to dominate the other jobs it does.

The appearance of inflation and deflation therefore marks periods in an economy when money is being increasingly treated as a means of exchange or a store of wealth respectively, and this tug-of-war is not predicated on zero inflation being understood as a stable state. The shifting sands of the urge to consume and the need to save are represented in the jobs money itself does, and therefore one is really looking at events affecting this relationship rather than assuming that a balance between the two is either optimal or even possible. A period of zero inflation, like a see-saw that is momentarily horizontal, is most likely a coincidence that we are tempted to idealise as a point of equilibrium. It is tempting to think of these monetary pressures primarily in terms of causality, such as banks lending too much or government fiscal policy leading to economic over-stimulation. One ought rather to think of inflation or deflation as events that show money speaking for itself, and that voice says either too much consumption relative to saving (inflation) or too much saving relative to consumption (deflation), and this often tends to be a question of whose hands the money is in (or is not, as the case may be).

Tracking the 'long-term' causes of bouts of inflation and deflation is notoriously hard, since one is ultimately asking what event caused a process to start, and this is the sort of question that lends itself to infinite regress. The inflation of the 1970s in the United States can be laid at President Nixon's feet for suspending the convertibility of the dollar to gold in 1971 (the 'Nixon shock'). Yet, in turn, this suspension could have been the result of the dual pressures in the previous decade of financing the Vietnam War and the Great Society project simultaneously. Equally, the inflationary pressures could be traced back to policies starting in the Kennedy presidency or to flaws in the 1944 Bretton Woods monetary settlement itself (notably the Triffin dilemma mentioned earlier) or even to inherent contradictions between the rising demands on the levels of government regulation and activity in modernity and the existence of strictly limited commodity-based money. The causality is really a question of how long one's memory is or how far back into history one wants to delve. There may be a number of reasons, but not necessarily one definitive cause.

Not only do we have to consider exogenous shocks like war or natural disaster, but we have to think about government policy both in purely fiscal terms (especially deficit spending), monetary terms (central bank interest-rate policy), as well as policy relating to the choice of monetary system itself. All of these can individually or collectively cause inflation or deflation, and this is what makes the causality so difficult to discern, especially given that there is not necessarily a start date. That money tells us when there is a problem is the only fact of which we can really be sure.

If inflation is an event, rather than something good or bad in itself, we may be better off asking, 'good or bad for whom?' Since inflation favours consumption over saving and thus reflects a bias towards money's job as a means of exchange over a store of wealth, it is clear that inflation favours debtors over creditors (borrowers over savers). When the US inflated away much of its war-debt after 1945, the situation in the US at the end of the war (rising productivity, high levels of growth, strong employment and rising wages) meant this inflation was not necessarily hammering the poor even as it helped a heavily indebted Federal government to ease its burden. Savers lost out but society 'generally did OK'. In other inflationary events (such as the 1970s, where real wages fell and unemployment was persistently high), the outcome was far less sanguine. The good and bad of inflation is therefore a relative matter and this often raises questions about wealth inequality.

Following the global financial crisis of 2007–9, global central banks took the lead from Japan's central bank and started a rolling programme of extraordinary monetary policy in the form of quantitative easing (QE), which involved a 'maturity swap' of buying longer-dated financial assets (mainly government debt, but also in some instances corporate credit and mortgage-backed securities) in the open market and replacing them with bank reserves (which are the most short-dated of assets). The knock-on effect of this was to force the bond sellers to reinvest elsewhere – most commonly in even-longer-duration or riskier assets. The new bank reserves were not automatically lendable and therefore did not result in higher bank lending (which would have had the knock-on effect of demand-driven inflationary pressures in the real economy).

The result of forcing investors into longer-duration or riskier assets, in the United States at least, was a phenomenon often described in the press as 'asset-price inflation'. The growing disparity in wealth between the rich and poor in the United States after the great recession has often been blamed on QE as manifested in asset-price inflation. A similar asset-price inflation phenomenon was observed in Japan in the late 1980s just prior to the crash, albeit in Japan's case this was an event driven by bank lending, not QE – Japan was a more homogeneous and less unequal society at the time and thus the benefits did not seem to be as unequally spread. In addition, the rage following the collapse seemed to be focused on the Japanese Ministry of Finance rather than the central bank (or the '1%') in this instance[11].

Yet asset-price inflation is a strange phenomenon. While it is described as 'inflationary', we do not talk about the assets concerned moving in an inflationary manner at a day-to-day level. If the price of bread or milk rose sharply in a given week we would instinctively call it inflation. Yet if the Dow Jones stock index were to rise by 2% on a given day, we don't say, 'the Dow inflated by 2% today', nor do we say, 'the Dow deflated by 500 points following poor employment data'. Yet, over the decade or so since the global financial crisis, the huge rise in the Dow Jones index is somehow explained in terms of asset-price *inflation*. If inflation is generally an event favouring the present over the future, where the desire to consume trumps the propensity to save, then QE in the United States arguably caused a type of back-to-front inflation that saw investors favour longer-dated or perpetual assets (like equities). Such investments are simultaneously riskier and therefore less stable, thus increasing the risk of adverse market events and sharp draw-downs in asset prices. This riskiness is arguably a sort of dangerous short-termism embedded in the long-termism of saving.

One might be better thinking that this QE-induced asset-price inflation is really an example of *reckless saving* – and that somehow such saving is short-sighted, especially if the assets purchased were bought at bubble-like prices that will at some point collapse. One is, however, on firmer ground if talking about how the compounding effect of wealth over time is a non-linear function, and central-bank QE illustrates the action of the Cantillon effect whereby different prices rise at different rates over time, favouring some (savers) over others (consumers), and how this forms the basis of a growing inequality in wealth. The sense of inequality and injustice is the event; the manner of the inflation that lies behind it is incidental.

Inflation is the sign of an excess of consumption relative to saving. One can look at this either as the prices of goods going up or the long-term value of money as a store of wealth falling. While one symptom of inflation is an excess of credit (hence too much money chasing too few goods), major inflationary episodes are often political in their origin.

Periods of inflation tend to manifest themselves where statutory controls on the government's influence on the money system (either in terms of the amount or the cost of money or both) are weak and where governments themselves are over-consuming capital through excessive fiscal deficits[12].

*   *   *

The relationship between government and money raises the question of the state theory of money, recently repackaged as modern monetary theory or MMT. While strong on the origin story of money, MMT does not necessarily show the limits of how money can be used or how it is valued by society. It also says little about the sources of lending (in the form of bank credit or private lending) within the economy. Yet, at the same time, modern governments' tendency to be the dominant entity in society and often in the economy means their role and influence deserve special attention. The state theory of money asserts that a country's money is a creation of the state, existing for the purpose of taxation[13]. From the technical perspective of legal tender, this is not in need of dispute and it is unsurprising therefore that territorial and monetary boundaries tend to be the same.

If an inflationary/deflationary equilibrium is not the theoretical starting point, then the object is not ascertaining a correct amount of money in the economy in the sense that any one entity (such as the government or central bank) can know what that equilibrium is. The occurrence of inflation or deflation domestically and appreciation and depreciation in the foreign-exchange market is money telling us about itself in terms not only of quantity but also qualitatively, particularly with respect to who has too much or too little of it. This might in turn be the starting point for confronting a view of economics where a steady state is seen as a norm or a target.

Proponents of modern monetary theory suggest that money creation for the purpose social goals, such as full employment or economic growth during periods of recession, is a legitimate use of the state's monopoly on the power to create money[14]. In form, this is no different from the behaviour governments exhibit during times of war except that spending on social projects such as benefits or entitlements often end up becoming perpetual in a way that wars, which end in peace, tend not to be. The war on want is one that never really ends.

However, the real questions are those of who creates the money, how much is created, and who gets it. That governments are the source of legal tender is one thing, but this does not mean that they are the only source of money in an economy; bank credit is a source of money with respect to this, even if banks' provision of credit is ultimately regulated by capital adequacy rules and reserve capital requirements. Through regulation of leverage ratios (the proportion of assets on a bank's balance sheet relative to its reserves and share capital) in the banking system, governments can control credit creation, but this job is considerably harder in an age where capital controls have been eroded and where non-bank lending has proliferated. In any case, in a free-market economy, these private-sector lending entities ultimately have a choice about how much they lend to whom and for how long.

In terms of the stock of debt, it is also worth noting how the amount of leverage in the global financial system has risen exponentially over the decades since the end of the Bretton Woods era and how, for much of this time, the rules relating to bank leverage (the Basel agreements) have been eased, at least relative to prior levels. When bank lending rules were tightened after the global financial crisis, government debt rose sharply to fill the gap left by bank and private-sector deleveraging. The common direction of travel following the 1971 suspension of gold convertibility under the Bretton Woods agreement, the easing of restrictions on capital controls and progress towards trade tariff reduction meant that increasingly credit could grow in a far more unchecked manner than before, flowing to wherever demand was appearing globally. While it didn't start in the 1970s, the process of financialisation clearly accelerated in that decade and was to progress further as globalisation picked up its pace during the 1990s with the end of the cold war and the 'opening up' of the Eastern Bloc and China. It went into overdrive as China was admitted to the World Trade Organisation (WTO) in 2001.

Rather than being a matter of human agency, it might therefore be better to think of money creation from the point of view of credit itself, in that the internal logic of the compounding of interest over time dictates that debt itself has to grow unless written-off or defaulted upon. In the fiat-money era, credit has simply been able to expand into territory previously restricted by the exogenous checks provided by a money system linked at some level to a metallic or commodity standard on the one hand, and other regulatory controls over lending and the international flow of capital and trade on the other.

Initiatives towards the long-term reduction of trade tariffs were promoted by the British a century before they were by the US, so the more recent version should be considered in the context of a post-second-world-war settlement promoted in the main by the United States. The coming together of rising capital and trade flows in the context of the post-Bretton-Woods, fiat-money era is the characteristic of the modern era of globalisation without being the cause of it. If money never sleeps, then the compounding of returns over time never stops. When free trade is promoted in the absence of capital controls alongside far fewer restrictions on lending *and*, critically, a fully flexible credit system of money, such as the post-1971 one, then financialisation through the growth of debt is essentially unstoppable.

Public-sector debt levels have risen sharply since the 1970s, and government activity ought to be considered both in the context of active moves towards financial liberalisation as well as the passive process of debt growth due to the compounding of interest. According to the state theory of money, government fiscal spending should only be bound by prudence with respect to avoiding rampant inflation[15]. The cure for this inflation is to raise taxes to reduce demand in the economy. This is clearly not always a politically opportune choice. In the representative government systems of the developed world, there is clearly a conflict of interests with respect to tempering inflation if the government in power is able to spend (or cut taxes) to help its own chances of election by favouring one constituency over another.

There is also a clear duration mismatch with governments elected for four- or five-year terms making policy based on actuarial calculations whose time horizons are often multi-decade. This is particularly true for economic decisions (or non-decisions) relating to pension retirement age, but is equally the case for environmental issues and foreign policy, the latter often gaining significance over multiple generations. It is potentially asking for too much restraint for a government seeking re-election or for an opposition seeking power to avoid making promises that win votes in the short term but demand a debasement of the monetary system in the long term due to unfunded or wasteful spending commitments. That governments seeking re-election (or dictators needing popular approbation) should be expected to show restraint with respect to spending is to demand the imposition of an exogenous rule where none exists.

The nineteenth-century gold standard was essentially a self-correcting system, which demanded from all participants (not just governments) a counter-cyclical approach to credit that saw interest rates and currencies rise and fall with the international flow of bullion through the economic cycle. The fiat-money system does not require this discipline, as currencies float against one another rather being bound together in a international framework such as the one provided by gold. Austerity is therefore, at most, a political choice (and usually a vote-losing one) not a systematic necessity. In such circumstances, political populism can quickly lead to inflation domestically and devaluation of the currency abroad. It is not the right or ability to act that is called into question; it is the monetary consequences that ought to be considered.

The tendency of hyperinflation to occur in fiat-money systems suggest that, left to their own devices and in the absence of sufficient statutory restraint with respect to money creation, governments lack either the restraint or the foresight to know when to switch the printing press off. One conclusion, therefore, might be that the state theory of money tends to emphasise money's role as a means of exchange to the detriment of its other roles, especially as a store of wealth. This is particularly true if government spending dominates, but it is also true of an excess in bank lending or private credit. A theory where money as a means of exchange and payment dominates over its role as a store of wealth makes money inherently inflationary. This means that practitioners of the state theory of money may find themselves confronted with an impossible task of avoiding inflationary consequences from a monetary philosophy promoting the most inflationary job that money can perform.

Without the self-enforced corrective mechanisms of the gold standard era, the fiat-money era is one with no real limits to the creation of money or credit. In the age of commodity-based money, the option of 'going to coin' (where one withdraws money from the banking system and keeps it as gold bullion in a safe) always meant that lenders, consciously or subconsciously, could leave an overly frothy market, thereby marking the top of the credit cycle. In the fiat-money era in which money is backed only by good faith, there is nothing out of which one can switch, and thus debt tends simply to keep on compounding (and public policy is then forced to aid and abet this process for fear of total financial collapse). Over time, this becomes deflationary as debt service costs builds up and, although the state might not need to default – since it has the power to print money as an alternative to taxing or borrowing, it nonetheless cannot escape the issue of the build-up of debt and eventually compromises the private (household or corporate) sector's ability to service it and therefore cannot avoid the ultimate inevitability of default. Money printing may mean defaults can be avoided by bail-outs, but this does not reduce the risk of devaluation of the currency abroad (against other fiat currencies) or against the suite of 'hard' commodities or consumer goods domestically. Either of these outcomes could result in runaway inflation as the domestic currency's value is rendered meaningless.

If money printing becomes habitual and therefore inflexible to the needs of the real economy, eventually imbalances between real levels of supply and demand emerge as the stock of money no longer equates to the amount necessary for it to function as a means of exchange. This is Gresham's Law, where bad money drives out the good. Another way of expressing this is that money ceases to have any value as a means of exchange and therefore its time-horizon is nil. In this instance, hyperinflation emerges, as money fails to function even as a tool for effecting consumption. While modern monetary theory can correctly lay claim to what it is possible for the state to do with respect to money, it cannot place itself outside the scope of the effect of the compounding of interest over time and the ensuing build-up of debt. Even keeping nominal interest rates at zero is not a solution for unchecked deficit financing and an ever-expanding stock of debt. Negative real interest rates ultimately make saving meaningless, eventually undermining the role of money as a store of wealth and ensuring the long-term destruction of capital within an economy through the tendency to promote malinvestment.

Controlling the price of money tends to mean an inability to control the quantity, and government deficit financing, aided by QE or the like, can result in the eventual crowding out of the private sector or the collapse of the currency in the foreign-exchange markets. More generally, any system relying on internal circumspection and moderation without external restraint in some form is ultimately liable to abuse, rendering its long-term viability questionable. This is where modern monetary theory falls short. Extremes of deflation or inflation are really a Hobson's choice in which money's role, either as a means of exchange or a store of value, ceases to operate in a meaningful way. When either happens, the ultimate consequence is that, eventually, money effectively dies.

★   ★   ★

The impact of a dominant or domineering executive on the monetary system tends to be inflationary in the short term, even if the political or geopolitical backdrop makes that situation a necessary one, particularly if national security is at risk. Governments tend to dominate by spending, and often co-opt the central banks to help this process by monetising fiscal deficits through the discounting of bills, QE or something equivalent. The advent of digital currencies, especially those organised and administered by central banks, potentially offers a new chapter in monetary history, but one whose outcome may not be all that new at all.

The prospect of citizens having bank accounts at the central bank throws up a number of possibilities. While the credit quality of a central bank is arguably higher than at a commercial bank (the former can create reserves so ought never to go bust), capabilities such as being able to add or take away money in people's accounts as a tool of policy is clearly a mixed blessing. While it offers efficiency in the case of distributions of cash (such as those necessitated during the lockdown in the 2020 pandemic), it also raises concerns about people's access to money and therefore goods and services if the same process were to go in reverse for political or partisan reasons. If money becomes a tool of control, then one wonders whether alternative options, especially those 'free' of government or central bank control, will prosper.

Central bank digital currencies (CBDCs) have been portrayed, at least in their theoretical stage, as tools for fine-tuning monetary policy. If there is a slowdown or a recession, money can easily be credited to bank accounts to be spent, and the motivation to spend can be enhanced by putting a time limit on using these new balances in a 'use it or lose it' fashion. Money with time limits is not a new departure. When cigarettes provided a key medium of exchange in the immediate post-war period in Germany (prior to the introduction of the Deutschmark in what was to become the German Federal Republic), the medium not only had a functional life span but was also clearly one that could be consumed[16]. The excessive churning of $1 US bills in Zimbabwe following the collapse of the Zimbabwe dollar in 2008 has led to the physical deterioration of the notes themselves, eventually meaning that they drop out of circulation[17].

It is, however, worth noting that these examples of money with a use-by date both come from countries experiencing crippling inflation. Perhaps this provides a cautionary note for policymakers, who must not only be able to judge precisely the output gap in the economy (the difference between its current and its potential productive capacity) into which a surge of money can be created without causing inflation, but also the much wider problem of unbalancing the value of money. If money is something to be got rid of due to some time limit, at what point does that process become embedded into the value of all money, permanently affecting the public's inflation expectations?

As with the discussion of the state theory of money, the key question for CBDCs is always one of restraint and the imposition of controls. If the creation of money through the provision of credit becomes the purview of the central bank (or the government via its central bank), it is quite possible that the commercial banking sector could wither or at least be undermined in this role. This would be particularly true if CBDC accounts at central banks offered to pay interest to retail customers, thus putting them into direct competition

with the commercial banking sector for those same customers' deposits. Not only could lending become uncommercial
or unprofitable, creating a bad debt problem for the economy
at large, it could also become entirely political in the manner
of the planned economies of the Soviet era.

As with the discussion of inflation and the state theory
of money, the problem is one relating to restraint, oversight
and accountability. It is not a simple argument of the market
being the best or only way to allocate resources, but one of
a single economic entity dominating the others to the detriment of all. That the jobs we require money to do makes
it inherently unstable is borne out by the history of monetary crises, particularly from the twentieth century onwards.
Technological and scientific advances have raised the material
standard of living for many, but the idea of making money
better or more efficient through new technology is perhaps
to misunderstand the necessary jobs which money does, since
they reflect the problems and questions lying at the heart of
the human economic experience. And, as they are recursive
by nature, they are not necessarily of the sort that lend themselves to one-off solutions.

5.

SAFETY IN NUMBERS: SAVING, INVESTMENT AND THE URGE TO COUNT

If the advocates of the state theory of money, discussed in the previous chapter, were looking for a foundation myth, what could be better than the image of the king in his counting house, stacking the money he minted, collected through the taxes he raised and to be spent as he decides? Clearly this is money being used the right way, if by right one means that money exists for the purpose of paying taxes. By contrast, the image of the miser sitting alone counting his money is an altogether different one. The personality traits of the miser are universally negative: avaricious, scrimping to the point of self-deprivation, a harmful excess of under-consumption or of over-saving and an ensuing lack of social interaction resulting in isolation bordering on the reclusive. In the same way that using a hundred-dollar bill to light a cigar is gratuitously wasteful, the miser's obsessive over-saving somehow creates that odd feeling that money is somehow being treated by them in the wrong way. If miserliness is saving the wrong way, does this mean there has to be a right way?

The discussion of sentimental value in Chapter 3 described it as a strictly personal matter outside the economic sphere. That something has a monetary value is shown by the possibility of that value being realised in the market by selling it. While the current value of a particular good or service can be approximated by its most recent market price, this is not to say that all individuals value things to the same extent. Nowhere is this truer than for a miser and his money. While the previous chapter discussed the value of money in terms of the roles it plays in economic decision-making, it only examined this in terms of the jobs we ask it do and how money's effectiveness at doing them can be assessed in terms of inflation or deflation, not as something with an inherent value in itself. In the case of the miser, the veneration of money is clearly not an activity in which money acts as a symbol of social status; miserly behaviour tends to be of the sort that results in social exclusion rather than an elevation in the hierarchy.

Being labelled a miser means not only an avaricious love of money itself, but loving it to excess. The implication is that when money is loved in this way, its accumulation over time is somehow different from 'normal' saving, since the miser's delaying of consumption (the intended purpose of saving) is accompanied not only by the absence of a lifestyle that would be typical for that level of wealth, but also a sort of perverse pride in self-deprivation, the failure to accede to the norms of hospitality and the like. One can at least understand why the king is in his counting house – perhaps he is assessing his revenues with the aim of building a new palace, waging a military campaign or something else that kings do. The miser, by contrast, is just counting and accumulating with no intention of ever spending. The accumulation is itself the goal, and as such is an intentional act. Both the king and miser are engaging in purposive action, but the apparent difference between what they are doing highlights the question of the relationship between counting and valuation, and also the role numbers play in this process.

When we are counting, we ask *how many?* When we are valuing, we ask *how much?* Counting is just about quantity, while valuation, as an ethical judgement, combines a sense of quantity *and* quality. If there is a confusion between counting and valuing, then it comes from the fact that both can keep score using numbers. On emptying one's piggy-bank, the piling of coins into uniform groups is an example of ranking – piles of ten coins for those who use a decimal system and so on. On its own, this is just a matter of counting[1]. Yet the very act of keeping a piggy-bank and then periodically counting out its contents suggests something else is also happening, of which the counting is only a part. Five piles of ten two-pence coins equals a pound, and this is a recognisable amount of money (salaries are after all paid in multiples of pounds, not two-pence coins). When one has gathered an amount of money rather than just a number of coins, one is saving rather than merely aggregating.

It seems strange to say that at some point, a number of coins becomes an amount of money. Is there really a moment at which the counting of coins stops and the measuring of an amount of money starts? The relationship between counting and valuing is in part a question about language rather than one of action. In English at least, the relative terms for amount and number overlap. There is a particular type of grammar obsessive (in Britain at least) who gets angry with supermarket checkouts set aside for those shoppers purchasing '5 items or less'. The rage comes from the observation that *less* is a measure of amount and *fewer* one of number. Since the items in a shopping basket are being counted in order to qualify for the fast-track checkout, the checkout aisles in question should be marked as '5 items or fewer', or so the pedants claim. There is clearly a confusion here between an amount of shopping and the number of items that the shopping comprises.

Such people might perhaps want to set aside their grammatical superiority for a moment to dwell on the fact that there is a genuine linguistic confusion here. While '*less* is to *amount* as *fewer* is to *number*' is a neat aide-memoire, it is also the case that '*more* is to *less* as *more* is to *fewer*', and this genuine overlap muddies the water between amount and number. Such confusion cannot happen for example in Latin, where the use of the partitive genitive makes clear that money is something measured as an amount (*satis pecuniae*, or 'enough of money'). In money terms, an object can be worth a certain amount in terms of value but also cost so many pounds or dollars to buy. We make a valuation but count the cost. Value and cost need not be identical in numeric terms, yet both are expressed numerically in terms of money. More importantly, as has been discussed in the previous two chapters, amount (value) and price (cost) exist simultaneously due to the way in which money performs its different functions as a system of account and a means of exchange.

Looking at valuing and counting in more detail, an example from the world of accounting is helpful. A stock take is an event where the amount of inventory a business holds is assessed. This is both an exercise in counting in terms of how many actual items there are in stock, and also one of valuation since accounting conventions demand the money-value of inventory items be assessed (FIFO or first in first out, LIFO or last in first out and so on). It is not simply the case of saying an 'amount of inventory' demands an answer in an aggregate like dollars our pounds. If one asked the owner of a car showroom how much inventory he was holding, he could say either $5,000,000 or 100 cars and be equally well understood. The answer to a question about an amount of inventory can be a number of items or an amount that they are worth. The confusion with money is that the number and the amount share the same unit, so one seems to be both counting and valuing simultaneously.

One way of describing accounting is to look at it as a stock take for all of a business's activity. It amounts to a periodic snapshot, usually taken quarterly or annually, where one is effectively dipping into a constant flow of transactions to create a moment at which all the operational and financial activities are measured. For companies whose equity is listed on the stock exchange, as well as being a legal requirement, the reporting of accounts is a key moment in the corporate news cycle. The company's management values the company on a periodic basis according to standard accounting rules. The very idea of accrual accounting and the matching process (where best practice involves the most honest balancing of the time-gap between when sales are made and the cash for them is actually received by the company) reflects the stylised nature of company accounts as a discrete measurement within the general flow of business a company is doing.

While quarterly and annual accounts are major events within the corporate calendar, nonetheless the stock market revalues the business on a daily basis if the company's equity is listed on an exchange. Because common equity is necessarily a standardised unit of value, the price is always set by the marginal buyer or seller, and this is done on a daily basis despite the infrequency of in-depth accounting updates on the overall business by management. The last-traded price acts as a value reference for owners, would-be buyers, sellers or potential short-sellers. This process is subjective – while it may be said that a company's shares move because of changes in a number of factors (company fundamentals, market sentiment, price technicals and macroeconomic concerns amongst others), the trader generally trades when his or her sense of value differs from the prevailing market one. One would not sell if one felt a stock was under-valued in a rising market, but one might buy more if the opportunity cost deemed it appropriate to switch investments.

The general sequence of actions in the market is as follows: event, reattribution of value, transaction (purchase or sale), price creation. The event itself can be trivial, such as the sensation of feeling hungry leading to the purchase of a sandwich.

As such, an event need not be considered as an active process or even a voluntary one. One does not choose to be hungry, nor does one necessarily choose to save a certain percentage of one's salary if there is legislation in place that requires compulsory retirement-investment contributions for example.

Action in the economic sphere generally occurs because someone either needs something or wants something. Even here, the distinction is not clear – I may need to eat because I am hungry, but I want a burger rather than a salad. Decisions of this sort are fairly trivial due to their frequency and low magnitude. Long-term decisions such as moving house or changing jobs are generally weighed far more seriously and, as such, the reattribution of value needed for the event to spur activity is far greater. Much in the same way a saver might not acknowledge the negative impact of a low but sustained level of inflation on the real value of money, so the absence of regular events of sufficient importance to spur a major revaluation probably explains why most investors do not turn over their whole portfolio every day. A lack of imagination wedded to an apparently firm belief that tomorrow will be like today to some extent explains the 'clustering' of investments into a fairly narrow range.

Most events relating to the reattribution of value are so trivial as to pass without notice. When I see that the best-before date on the milk in the refrigerator has passed, I have to take stock of my needs and wants. I need two pints and prefer semi-skimmed. In terms of counting and value, two is the number of pints of milk equating to the amount of milk I estimate I need before it goes sour or runs out. Price discovery is also trivial in this sense – one person's needs do not affect the global or even the local level of milk prices, nor does one normally haggle for a better price for a pint of milk at the supermarket.

The impact of aggregate demand, supply, monetary inflation and the like dictates the overall price paid, but the very commoditisation of some goods, itself the result of the frequency of consumption, makes the process of reattribution of value and price discovery into a seemingly passive one or at least a remote one where it is not exactly obvious to the individual what is actually happening or what their impact is with respect to aggregate demand. Although they can at times be described as such, consumers rarely feel themselves to be doing the job of price-taker or price-setter. Every pay rise contributes to inflation in its own little way, but the aggregate national inflation rate is probably the last thing on the individual's mind when he or she is having this particular discussion with the boss. This is because economic valuation is an individual act about something that matters collectively.

We tend to talk about the things we consume in terms of them being cheap and expensive rather than over-valued or under-valued, judging them by comparison with their cost in the past. If a price changes dramatically, it looks like either a bargain or a rip-off. Even the Thomist idea of the 'just price' (the concept put forward by St Thomas Aquinas that prices should be agreed in light of the wellbeing of those involved in the transaction as well as the community at large) is one where a price for something like grain is judged as being fair based on memory or experience[2]. This is still largely true of durable goods that can be resold, though housing is also often spoken of in terms of being affordable or unaffordable for certain groups in society rather than being judged by any sense of intrinsic worth. Housing affordability, itself a relative term, is often measured through another relationship: that of average house prices to average income.

When we make consumption decisions, we have a sense of whether goods are cheap or expensive based on past prices. By contrast, when we talk about things being over-valued or under-valued, we need a fair value against which to compare it. For investment, we tend to have in mind a price target (or fair value) in the future, even if that target is itself based on our experience of the past. This marks a key distinction in valuation between consumption and saving. Financial investment (the allocation of savings) lends itself to the use of fair values, as it is inherently concerned with future worth, in a way that the immediacy of the act of consumption does not.

In a sense, the distinction between goods and investments is an artificial one, as an object's status is really only defined by the event of valuation, and that is particular to time and place. One might argue that antiques are an example of objects that are both good and investment at the same time. This is nominally true if one thinks it worth paying a huge premium for a regency dining table over the price one might pay for a more modest version bought on the high street. You can eat your dinner off both, but only one is likely to have retained its value or even appreciated fifty years hence.

What one is really saying is that some objects retain their value better than others, in the sense discussed in Chapter

3 with respect to the difference between what the collector collects and the hoarder hoards. It may sound absurd to say that a fancy dining-room table is an investment (for the future) when one buys it but is transformed into a good (for use in the present) when one sits around it for Sunday lunch, but this shows how the event of valuation defines the nature of the object. Use, or the more general idea of utility, cannot provide the full answer to this question, even if utility encompasses the idea of displaying social status or wealth. Clearly it is the event of valuation that matters more, and this is an ongoing and *situational* process.

To illustrate the issue further, one could use the example of silver, a metal now used mainly for either industrial purposes or for jewellery, which also has a long history as a monetary metal. When we talk about 'the family silver', we have in mind cutlery, utensils and other flatware of the sort now generally used on special occasions but that, in former times, was used on a daily basis by the well-to-do. Yet, given the term's idiomatic meaning as a multi-generational store of wealth, it seems odd to think of the family silver as an investment when it is stored in the sideboard but a good when it is laid out on the table. For insurance purposes, there is clearly no difference. Perhaps this confusion is a hangover from when banking was in its infancy and silver utensils were a key store of wealth. The idea of 'selling the family silver' is now just a euphemism for the imprudence of liquidating assets for short-term need, but its sense comes from a time when money was metallic and when silver plate was melted down to form coins when the need arose. The physical transformation of plate to coin is symbolic of the shift from silver as a store of wealth to a means of exchange and therefore from the future to the present.

We should not be confused by the fact that we now think of silver coins as a store of wealth. That would be an anachronism. If one wants to understand the deep psychology of inflation, one ought first to look at how silver is used (and therefore valued), not at its physical form. 'Selling the family silver' is an act of liquidation usually associated with desperation, and if this meant melting down heirlooms into coins to exchange for goods then one ought to consider the shift from silver as store of wealth to silver as means of exchange as an inflationary act, with a shift in the investment horizon from the future to the present. Turning plate to coin to buy land or to invest in some other business venture would be an entirely different exercise.

Because we are presented with an ongoing and recursive choice between consumption and saving, our sense of value as a time horizon is constantly shifting between the present and the future. That we like to fix definitions and feel that we stand on solid ground with respect to terminology does not help our understanding of this process. While goods and services relate to consumption in the present on the one hand and investments relate to saving and the future on the other, the actual objects we value appear to be able to slide between good and investment depending on the circumstances in which they are valued. This mutability is usually the unseen object of commentators who object to excesses of speculation. When one hears critics of the financial markets railing against speculation and short-termism, there appears to be an implicit understanding that the idea of saving is being subverted and that what ought to be an activity with a view to the long term is one that is being dragged into the present, with all the risks of volatility, market crashes and so on that go with it.

If one were to ask the same critic of short-termism what the *right* holding period for a particular investment was, all they could probably say would be 'longer than what is happening currently'. There *is* no correct answer to this question, since the right length of time is a value judgement specific to the economic agent at that time. This echoes the difference between Newton's conception of measurement of time being correct (always true) and Einstein's idea of such measurements being proper (appropriate to the body concerned). What they could say with more authority is that the sort of use of financial leverage that accompanies periods of excessive short-termism and speculation, particularly with respect to retail investors borrowing on margin to buy shares, effectively amounts to an act of consumption, since the use of leverage through credit implies drawing consumption from the future into the present. That the money is then often invested in risky assets or at high levels of valuation is just an example of reckless saving. The use of margin debt puts short-term pressure on long-term investments like equities due to the problem of meeting margin calls and the like.

Criticising the use of leverage when buying shares is only a comment on the risks of short-termism. It still doesn't tell us the *correct* length of time to hold an investment. In

addition, periods of excessive speculation are often characterised by the extensive use of financial derivatives – call options
in particular, which provide leveraged returns when prices
rise. This phenomenon (the use of leverage, both in terms
of credit and through financial derivatives) has been true of
all recorded bubbles, back to the Dutch tulip mania of the
1630s[3]. The riskiness of speculating using financial derivatives
such as options comes from their hybrid form of being long-
term savings instruments (equity) with the best-before date
(option expiry date) of a consumable good. The leveraged
returns achievable from the use of options or other derivatives compensates for the compressed time period in which a
desired price outcome must occur.

*   *   *

In financial markets, option-pricing theory breaks down the
value of an option into several components known as 'the
Greeks', since they are signified by letters from the Greek
alphabet like delta and gamma. Theta is the 'Greek' used
to signify the time-value of an option. Since most common
option-pricing models are probability-based, the closer one
gets to the expiry of a particular option contract, the lower
the probability that the option expires in-the-money for a
profit. The decay of the theta (or time-value) of an option as
it approaches maturity is not a linear function; most of the
decay happens in the final portion of an option's 'life', and
that decay is exponential to zero as expiry approaches. If a
call option, which represents the right to buy, expires below

its strike price (the price at which the option confers the right to transact), it expires worthless. The same is true when a put option, representing the right to sell, expires above its strike price. It doesn't so much 'trade' at a price of zero as expire at zero value – once again, this shows how price and value are two separate phenomena. The value of an option expiring in-the-money comes from the intrinsic value of being able to buy or sell at a favourable, off-market price (the strike price) versus the current market price.

The key component to valuing an option is the volatility of the underlying security or instrument on which the option is written. Volatility is a measure of how much a price is likely to move in a given period of time, where high volatility means large expected price movements. In financial parlance, volatility, otherwise known as the standard deviation of returns, is the square root of variance, which is in turn the average of the squared deviation from the mean (average) return in the sample period. Even for those not *au fait* with option theory, the meaning of the word volatility is clear: the more volatile something is, the bigger the price moves and the 'riskier' it is.

The calculation of option volatility (in the widely used Black-Scholes model at least) is based on the idea of the random walk, the idea that at any stage a price is as likely to go up as it is down. In physics, this is the principle behind Brownian motion. Variance, from which volatility is derived (volatility is the square root of variance), calculates the dispersion (or range) of individual price observations from the mean (or average) in the period being measured. At any particular increment in the random walk, the variance is proportional to the time during which the observed data point was moving. Volatility is the square root of variance and is proportional to the square root of time, since the square root of a product of two numbers is equal to the product of their square roots.

What these mathematical relationships mean is that the volatility or riskiness of any given security or financial instrument is calculated by assessing how much its price moves during a given period of time, and that volatility is proportional to time (in fact the square root of time). If all living things need to consume to survive, but humans alone save on a voluntary basis because of their awareness of the future, then the clearest way of quantifying this conception of time is to look at how we actually value the change in our time horizon. If changes in our perception of the value of time lead to changes in price (in the sense that we go into the market to transact), then the volatility of the prices of the things we transact in reflects the speed at which our sense of present and future are moving relative to one another. In this sense, option volatility is a measure of the speed at which our investment time horizon is expected to shorten or lengthen at any given time.

In the financial markets, periods of high volatility reflect extreme change and uncertainty, with lower levels of volatility generally reflecting calmer periods. That the volatility of call options (the right to buy) is generally lower than of put options (the right to sell) in the equity market shows that the movements in time horizon from the present to the future and back are not always equal in pace. The difference between call and put volatility is called the 'skew' in market parlance, and a 'positive' skew exists between puts and calls when put volatility is more expensive on a relative basis. That skew tends to be positive for equities, for example, suggests that markets always tend to fall faster and more dramatically than they rise, all else being equal. The so-called term structure of volatility, how implied (future estimates of) volatility changes when we use different time horizons to measure it, also shows that volatility tends to be higher over a longer time horizon, reflecting an increase in uncertainty of outcome.

The periods of high volatility we see when markets fall sharply shows the foreshortening of the aggregate investor time horizon happening at a much faster pace than the gradual rise in confidence as that same investor time horizon extends. As they say, the market takes the escalator up but the elevator down. Once again, periods of low volatility reflect high liquidity, and liquidity here means agreement on price but disagreement on value (as discussed in Chapter 3). The high volatility one sees in a market crash is a perverse example of everyone agreeing that it is time to sell, but no one having much conviction of the value of buying at that particular price point. Conversely, a sharp rise in a company's equity price when a takeover bid is made for it reflects a sudden revaluation of the stock based on new facts, with the price adjusting accordingly.

The increasing frequency of destabilising events in the financial markets suggests that financial derivatives are a key source of instability in the global financial system due to the leverage embedded within them and the potentially large profits and losses these can cause in times of stress. This is particularly so in adverse scenarios where market participants find themselves on the hook for large pay-outs due to events that are supposed never to happen. Yet the growth of the derivatives market, particularly the volume of derivatives that trade relative to their underlying instruments (derivatives get their name from deriving their value from another, under-lying, financial instrument), can be seen as a key development in the increasing sophistication of markets with respect to the valuation of time itself. This has only been possible with the huge advances in computing power in the past forty or so years, which has permitted a new level of mathematical sophistication to enter the financial markets to price these derivatives accurately and continuously.

Beyond the technological aspect, the overall liberalisation of the capital markets and the reduction in capital controls are the other key contributors to the growth in the global deriv-atives market. The rise in the overall global stock of debt is the other consequence of the financial, regulatory and trade reform characterising the last half century or so. The expan-sion of global derivatives markets and the rise in the overall global stock of debt are often described as symptoms of the trend towards the financialisation of the global economy.

If, however, one looks at debt as borrowing time and finan-cial derivatives as in some sense pricing time, then one is as well to talk about the temporalisation of the global economy as opposed to its financialisation. The growing frequency of financial market crises, and the increasingly aggressive fiscal and monetary responses employed to deal with them, perhaps reflect a degree of volatility within the process of financialisation itself.

At one end of the economic time horizon is the immediacy of the now and at the other is the boundlessly optimistic future we contemplate during the soaring heights of a stock market bubble. This is quite a range. At one end there is our next meal and at the other the parabolic price movements that characterise manias over tulips or dot-com stocks (or more recently 'meme stocks'), which are the very cliché of 'blue-sky thinking'. In terms of time, the sort of vertiginous price rises witnessed during stock market bubbles reflects a view of almost never-ending profit growth over an almost-boundless time horizon. Valuation is thus bound at one end by the instant and at the other by the infinite.

With respect to the relationship between price and value, it is notable that there are few if any examples of prices rising infinitely. The periodic failure of monetary systems leads to massive price increases in goods and services within the domestic economy (inflation), but this is really a case of a currency collapsing and becoming worthless and investors' or consumers' time horizons declining to hand-to-mouth durations. There can be no clearer example of this than anecdotes of housewives in Weimar Germany during the inflation of the early 1920s queuing outside factories to get their husbands' wages during the day in order to buy food as the prices were moving with unimaginable rapidity even on an hour-by-hour basis. A few million percentage points of inflation may be the difference between a nearly worthless and a completely worthless currency but, nonetheless, these changes grab our attention in an almost prurient way.

*   *   *

Economic expansions or big stock-market rallies share the language of growing confidence. These periods are regularly described in terms of 'climbing the wall of worry' and the like. This is not so much that people know what the future holds, more that the degree of belief or certainty with respect to how long the good times will continue into the future is rising. The counterbalancing emotions of confidence and doubt (or greed and fear) are analogous to the idea of an expanding or shrinking collective economic time horizon marking out the various stages of the economic cycle.

When examining how periods of rising valuation start, develop, taper and then reverse, equity indices provide a useful if imperfect reflection of the level of confidence in how a nation's economy is going to perform. Shares price on a daily basis and thus offer an excellent empirical record of these changes in mood. By convention, equity investors use long-term fundamental valuation multiples of earnings and cash-flows to create price targets or trading ranges within which they feel comfortable buying or selling. The most common valuation multiple for equities is the ratio of price to earnings (the P/E ratio). A high P/E multiple means a company's stock is trading at a high price relative to its earnings. The earnings in question can be historical or estimates for the future. A high P/E ratio, particularly if that ratio is high versus its own long-term average, means that, all else being equal, the owners of the stock believe that future company earnings will be high relative to their own history for a considerable period of time. The higher the ratio, the stronger the belief.

The common market practice of relating a stock's current P/E ratio with its own long-term average reflects another core element of valuation in financial markets: that of reversion to the mean or average. This is easy to describe numerically in terms of price; a stock with a current P/E ratio too high or low relative to its own long-term average multiple will eventually move to a level reflecting that mean over a long-enough time period. This reflects an idea that abnormally high or low earnings cannot persist in a competitive and free economy unless there is a monopoly or oligopoly.

In financial analysis, company profitability, especially the mean-reversion of supra-normal profits over time (due to external pressure such as competition, substitution, rising costs and the like) is the key axiom for valuing companies by metrics such as the P/E ratio. Especially for mature companies with more stable earnings streams, the phenomenon of stock prices rising relative to earnings is called multiple expansion and is usually seen as reflecting rising confidence. If this higher valuation persists, one could say that shareholders believe the company will earn supra-normal profits for an extended period of time. Excessive valuations can be viewed as dangerous. For example, should a mature business trade at a P/E ratio of twice its own long-term average, one might call this overvalued and expect the shares to underperform over time. This can be the case even for solid companies with stable business models. As the old saying goes, when buying shares, price is what is you pay but value is what you get – overvalued companies tend to underperform in price over the long term.

An alternative way of interpreting a high company P/E relative to its own long-term average is that it says something about valuation in terms of time and, more importantly, investors' current time horizons. Equities as an asset class are sometimes described as a long-term call option (the right to buy) on a company's cash-flows, and are perpetual so long as the company exists (or the equity listing exists). Conventionally speaking, a high P/E suggests not only potential earnings surprise versus historical averages and especially future estimates, but also, because of the nature of equity as a quasi-perpetual asset class, that these abnormal earnings will continue over an extended period of time.

A clearer way of looking at the phenomenon of high P/E ratios is to see investors' time horizon for rising company profits being extended out into the future. The catalysts for this new-found confidence can be endogenous (relating to a narrative specific to the company or industry in question) or exogenous (for example, favourably easy central-bank monetary policy or tax cuts). What this fails to fully explain, though, is that the stock market tends to trade on a high multiple at the top of an economic expansion and a low one at the trough of a recession. Corporate earnings rise and fall with the economic cycle, but it is in the variation in earnings multiples, especially at an equity index level, where the peaks and troughs in the overall investor time horizon can best be observed. In this sense, investor confidence, especially in riskier and more volatile asset classes such as equities, is really a measure of confidence in the future *as viewed from the present*.

The apparently excessively high equity valuations of 'disruptive' companies or those in new industries with 'new rules' (such as the dotcoms in the late 1990s) often reflects the vaulting hopes of investors. Without any real experience of this type of company or industry to provide a historical analogy, hopes of infinitely rising profits can elevate stock prices only for reality eventually to reign-in such outlandish hopes. Similarly, one way of explaining the mean reversion of companies' P/E ratios to their long-term average is that investors' time horizon for excess profits eventually starts to shrink as the reality of how the business actually performs becomes clearer, and it is during this period of time that the 'gravity' of competition, regulation, input costs and the like make themselves more apparent and better understood to the market. In market parlance, this is usually described as good news being increasingly 'priced-in'.

Clearly, such a change in time horizon is not instantaneous and is better understood as a progression, but one that progresses at a varying pace (and that can turn back on itself at various points). Efficient market theory does not explain this phenomenon, relying as it does on the idea of instant corrections to share prices as new news appears in the market rather than an ongoing fluctuation in investors' time horizons. The concept of investors' ever-changing time horizons and the varying pace at which they move can perhaps best be illustrated at the very opposite end of the scale from a bubble-like stock valuation. Taking the quip sometimes attributed to Mark Twain that bankruptcy happens very slowly then all at once, it is the perception of time and the time horizon changing that most readily explains the sense of this aphorism. The time (or perception of it) being described here is clearly not linear but geometric. The sudden and precipitous decent into bankruptcy is identical to the pattern discussed above relating to the decline in the time-value (theta) of options as they approach expiration at maturity.

Apart from legal considerations with respect to the corporate capital structure, equities differ from bonds in the sense that the latter tend to have a maturity date on which the principal is returned while the former are tradeable so long as the company exists as an exchange-listed entity. Given that the maturity, redemption price and coupon are generally fixed, when one buys a bond, one knows one's nominal (non-inflation adjusted) return over the life of the investment at the point of purchase. Because equity is essentially perpetual, its value reflects to a great extent the confidence of the marginal investor at any given point in time. At very high P/E valuation multiples for example, one might say that the marginal investor expects tomorrow to be like today for an extended period of time, perhaps all the way to their ultimate investment horizon (retirement, or some other far-away point). The degree to which this is the case could be described as confidence or bullishness.

At the top of a bull market, therefore, investors have a long time horizon and are very confident. At the depths of a recession, amid unemployment and corporate insolvencies, their time horizon is very short. In this sense, equities being over- and under-valued on a valuation-multiple basis becomes a judgement on the value of time. Time is itself the variable, and it varies geometrically rather than in a linear fashion. One way of assessing time itself as a variable is therefore to look at the relationship between historical levels of asset-price volatility versus their current implied level based on the market prices of various options, especially in the context of the credit and capex cycles (as discussed in the previous chapter).

★   ★   ★

Both equity shares and commodity futures are standardised and are usually listed so that one can easily tell what the market thinks they are 'worth' at any given point. Yet, while investors have fair values for equities, it sounds very odd to ask what the fair value for milk or oil is. We may think the price of oil is going to rise or fall in the future, but that is to say something different about likely future demand and supply factors. Because of their peculiar nature as quasi-perpetual securities, equities lend themselves to the idea of a fair value.

The fair value of shares amounts to a subjective view of what a company's equity is worth, and it may or may not be the same as the price at which one can trade the shares in the market on a particular day. For long-lived instruments like equities, there is time enough for that view of value to be realised in a way that does not exist for commodity futures, since the latter have fixed maturity dates requiring physical delivery (and therefore presumably consumption). A broken clock tells the right time twice a day, but its time is only known to be 'correct' when a functional time-piece validates it – and then only for an instant. In the same way, for any market participant, a stock's fair value is only really 'correct' at the moment the market price validates it as the same. The idea of fair value is therefore a subjective one derived from the investor's own time horizon, sometimes coincident to the market price but always dependent upon it as a reference point.

A particular view of the future is therefore implicit in the activity of saving, and investment is the means by which we express that view. In this framework, the reattribution of value can therefore be seen as the process by which our individual sense of value, based on experience and realised through personal circumstances, which are subject to continuity and change, alters within an overall framework of shared values. While our opinions about value are our own, the mediums through which they are expressed (shares, bonds, real estate and so on) are shared and therefore subject to trends affecting the economy in general while affecting the individuals that comprise it at the same time, only at a different pace and to a different degree at any given point. This is again quite different to the idea behind the efficient market hypothesis that suggests new information is priced the instant it is received by 'the market'.

If investors' sense of value changes enough, they are brought to market to trade. This threshold to action is itself not a fixed one. Technological changes in markets, which have meant a shift from open-outcry of dealers in a trading pit at an exchange to the ability now to trade from one's mobile device, have clearly made expressing a view on the market easier, and the growth of markets globally (particularly the reduction in capital controls) has meant the range of financial instruments available to the average investor has grown. Those critics of short-termism in the market would do well to dwell on the issue of how technology has reduced the average investment holding period in much the same way as fast food or microwaves have changed eating habits over the years.

In order to trade, those in the market have, by necessity, to agree a price. In addition, their strength of opinion about how different their own sense of value is from the currently tradable market price dictates the amount they are willing to trade at any given moment. Thus, the relationship between trading volumes and price volatility, often described as *liquidity*, becomes a question of the level of disagreement over value. Liquidity ought therefore to be considered as an asset class in itself, albeit a partially qualitative one, and one reflecting the degree of willingness with which market participants express their implicit disagreement with one another over value. That disagreements over value lead to trading and thus price formation means that trading volume is most meaningful when considered in terms of the volatility of prices, and since volatility is an expression of time, value and time show themselves to be inextricably linked with respect to the market and activity within it.

The reasoning and sentiment behind the valuation ultimately driving trading varies over time and with fashion. Increasingly, environmental and social causes are measures by which corporate management are judged and therefore by which shares are valued. Looking at a historical price series for a company's equity shows us how it was valued in the past, against both its current market price or relative to other firms over time. It does not say anything about why we valued it or what we valued it for. While prices are empirical facts and tell us the value-history of a particular asset or instrument in price terms, they say nothing about the reasons for the judgement, only that it was changing in a certain way in price terms.

⋆ ⋆ ⋆

One development highlighted by technological advance, and growing computing power in particular, is that we increasingly seem to value numbers (especially in the form of prices series) for qualities of their own. If one is valuing a company based on its earnings, then a high earnings-multiple valuation can be justified if supra-normal profits are being made and this state of affairs is expected to continue for some time. If one is analysing a relatively open and competitive economy, then one may infer that, over time, these supra-normal profits will normalise. Porter's five forces (rivalry amongst existing competitors, new entrants to the segment, supplier power, buyer power and substitution) offer a combination of themes that can explain the rise and fall of corporate profits over time and which justify the idea of assuming a mean reversion to average levels of profitability over a long enough interval. These are phenomena in the real economy.

What is quite different is the way many systematic and algorithmic trading strategies focus in general terms on the numeric properties of price series, particularly standard deviation, mean reversion and the measuring of the volatility of these trends as things in themselves, divorced from the real economy. In a way, prices become the subject of their own meta-valuation as numbers changing in time. This is of course not new – the nature of financial bubbles over the centuries has been one where staggering price moves bely a fascination with numbers beyond the conventional role of price as a record of value. That numbers can get so big so quickly is an enticement on its own and reflects the 'quick' element of the 'get rich quick' lure of financial bubbles, where numbers are increasingly valued for the speed at which they change. The same phenomenon is true during periods of very high inflation or hyperinflation. Rapid numeric change has an allure and therefore a value of its own, for good or ill.

While price series have always described patterns, it often seems that the abstract, logical parameters of mathematics as observed in prices is now a quality that is valued far more than it used to, at least on a short-term basis. That share-price movements often appear, for example, to be affected by the likes of 50-day or 200-day moving averages or Fibonacci ranges is not really so different from saying that centuries are important to cricketers or hat-tricks to footballers. They may be considered as noteworthy events within the game or landmarks in an individual player's career, but they are only contingent if nonetheless psychologically important contributions to the final result of the match, and that match, and the league within which it is played, is ultimately one of value not price.

While purely quantitative trading strategies are very much the product of the computer age, the lure of the numeric has been far more enduring within economics over time. In terms of counting, the wild success of Indian place-value notation along with Arabic notation of the zero as both null and cypher has led to this counting system gaining a universality far beyond anything a language has ever achieved[4]. Latin perhaps came close in mediaeval Christendom, but that ought probably to be thought of as a largely closed society, and one in which only the well-educated were participants. The 'Globish' version of English might stake a claim today, but one would hesitate to bet on this being so in a few centuries time, notwithstanding the current, dominant language of the internet being English.

The scientific urge to count, measure and seek generality through pattern-finding is fertile ground for considering prices (and therefore numbers) as the empirical facts of the economic sphere. The trifecta of computing power, economic globalisation and market deregulation has in some ways ensured the primacy of this price-focused method of analysis, both in economics and in financial markets.

It is tempting to think that the same abstraction that lends mathematics its universality can also do so for economics, as both share a numeric foundation, with economics doing so with prices. To say this is not the case is not to decry statistical analysis – far from it. What is critical is to define the boundaries of economics' claims to generality, and thus to understand the conditional nature of what one can say beyond these limits. This is particularly true when making predictions about the future based on the past. Mathematics may be a universal language but its very abstraction is a contrast to the economic sphere, which is particular in place and time. To treat prices just as numbers is to ignore their relationship with value and their location in time.

If one considers prices as historical facts, the way one uses them in economics is more akin to the best practice in history, where the quality of one's argument is judged as much by the honesty of one's approach with respect to the treatment of the evidence as it is currently accepted and presented as it is by the argument's own internal logic. The internal coherence of an historical argument is subordinate to, but also contingent upon, its correspondence to the external facts – or to what are known to be or accepted as the facts at that point.

For economics as well as financial market analysis, there is a temptation to use prices (as a record of the past) as a predictive tool with far more confidence and especially more precision than historians might use the past to predict the future course of events. There are of course exceptions in history, notably the determinist approach of Marxist historians, but it is interesting that this approach makes claims to being scientific that are not dissimilar to the way in which economics seeks perhaps to locate itself closer to the hard sciences than the social ones, especially with respect to economics' powers of induction. This is true also of financial market analysis, especially technical approaches to price analysis such as charting.

It is ironic that while pattern-finding is such a widespread and thus crucial way of analysing financial market performance, nonetheless financial products (in the UK at least) bear the provision that *past performance is no guide to future returns*. That certain economic events are recursive does not make them predictable, let alone cyclical.

Statistical methods, while valid as a tool of historical analysis, say as much about how we value numbers and their organisation as they do about the probability of future events happening in a certain way. The abiding lesson of behavioural economics is quite how 'bad we are at numbers' in everyday situations. It is tempting to dismiss this as irrationality and by doing so pave the way for a rational, economic man to clean up (both in markets and predictions for the economy). Perhaps homo economicus only exists in this abstract world of numbers where everything works in theory. It may also be the case that the nature of how we treat prices is being changed by the medium of money itself. The inexorable rise of debt on the one hand and the increasing frequency and magnitude of central-bank interventions in the economy on the other, both characteristics of the fiat-money era, have arguably weakened our sense of money as numeraire or an abstract measure of value (see Chapter 4), making money into an increasingly meaningless numeric game.

The role price plays in fortifying economists and market analysts with confidence about prediction comes from its numeric nature, and this allows mathematics to be used to create coherence (patterns) out of historical economic data that would likely not happen if that data were in another format. It is probably not coincident that astrology as a means of prediction was and is heavily reliant upon mathematics[5]. Written evidence in history, for example, does not lend itself to the same type of categorisation and, while patterns none-theless emerge, one can hold no more than an opinion about whether this is repetition or rhyming. Rather than dealing in terms of probability, the best one can aim for in history is a qualitative analysis about the veracity and insight of a partic-ular source – its value.

One cannot deduce whether history actually repeats itself or necessarily induce what will happen in the future from that which has happened before. History sadly tends to be far too lesson-free. Nor can one say with any confidence whether those future events will have the same significance as those from the past they superficially resemble. History lacks a strict measure of testability that would allow it to lay strong claim to being scientific. With no test environment, there is no way of proving if an argument is wrong. Its claim to the truth therefore relies heavily on the honesty and integrity of historians themselves with respect to the treatment of source material, especially where newly unearthed information is used to challenge currently accepted views or theories. If economics' claim to empiricism lies in the historical record of prices, this would suggest that such historiographical lessons are equally applicable to the sphere of economics and the financial markets.

If history is defined as an exercise undertaken in the pres-ent to find meaning in the past using what evidence has been left to us, its predictive claims thus appear more immediately

limited as the purpose of history is not necessarily an inductive one. In addition to the ethical aspects of best practice,
history's claim to truth stems from the very activity itself as
an exercise in understanding the past from the perspective of
the present. That this activity can be meaningful relies heavily
on the sense that there is enough of a shared human experience over the centuries to allow the historian to interpret
past events on their own terms and also to relate these events
to the present in a coherent form that is true both to past
and present simultaneously. This goes far beyond memory
and record. If prices are a record of value, then events such
as the South Sea Bubble of 1720, the British railway bubble
of the 1840s and the dotcom bubble of the late 1990s can all
be drawn together as showing that we value things, sometimes to excess, and that these extreme events all had much in
common (especially the excess use of credit). The exact price
moves are not the thing to be compared beyond their obvious
abnormality, nor do they allow for predications about where
and when the next bubble will emerge.

It is in the very fact that these bubbles are remembered
as events that they acquire their historical significance, in
this case within the genre of financial market history. In the
same way that the demographic categorisation of household
formation under the headings *Birth*, *Death* and *Marriage* gives
no sense of the infinite variety of the human experience, so
saying all financial bubbles have such-and-such a character
does not answer the question of why on earth the Dutch
thought those tulip bulbs were worth so much at that particular time. As with Solomon saying there is nothing new under

the sun, so categorisation of events into types or sets may be the way in which history seems to repeat itself. One could go as far as to say history simply *looks like* it repeats itself because there are only so many things that can actually happen. The present (the now) is a discrete and local event itself, not some sort of shifting but continuous viewing-box. In economics, to consider price without value is to make the same mistake not only of inferring too much from the particular to the general but of abstracting our view of the past from its locus in the present.

Although ultimately based on price series as a form of historical record, it sometimes seems that economic or market history is somehow less rigorous, not least because it contains narratives about people and policy as well as just numbers. Those branches of economics with a more mathematical and statistical focus are, by contrast, perceived to be more 'robust' and powerful, as they seem to be able to make a greater claim to generality than the historical approach of merely stringing events together into a coherent narrative. Price series in different countries at different times are thus easy to compare, and this means comparison on a like-for-like basis. The very abstraction of mathematics lends this type of statistical analysis to pattern-finding and then to rule-making. Rather than the conception of history presented earlier, where the interpretation of the past from the present acknowledges a sequence of events through time made meaningful by a shared human experience, the pattern-seeking and rule-making tendencies in economics ironically calls on an older conception of history.

The idea of *historia magister vitae* (history as the teacher of life) is one that fits far more closely to economics' pretensions to predicting the future, where past events were used as direct comparisons to guide future behaviour. Prior to the Enlightenment and the pursuit of human self-improvement, and the counter-trending ideas of the likes of Vico and Herder with respect to history being a progression through time, the events of ancient Greece and Rome had a sense of immediacy to the early modern mind that is hard to contemplate today[6]. In Europe in the early modern period, it was perhaps the millenarian tendencies of Christianity and the perceived proximity of the end of days that foreshortened the centuries and allowed similarities with past ages to be explored and revered despite the obvious differences[7].

The extreme compression of time – stories of the ancients as a guide to how we should behave today – mirrors mathematics' abstract and atemporal character, and it is perhaps this propensity to abstraction that enables mathematics to play this key role in economics with respect to predicting the future, creating precision with respect to a view of things to come where the discipline of history suggests there is none. Prices play the roles once occupied by kings, tyrants and heroes of antiquity, providing models of behaviour and a guide to action. Modern computing power has only intensified this trend, and with it, an emphasis on similarity rather than difference, homogeneity rather than heterogeneity. Market activity becomes a serial event where the emphasis on statistical analysis and pattern-seeking becomes an end in itself, which increasingly leaves prices simply as numbers that change. Whether it is people or machines that are doing the valuing in this instance is open to question.

★ ★ ★

Looking at price series from an entirely statistical perspective captures some of the significance of price movements but necessarily misses out on much. Financial bubbles show us that we are subject to manias and that the excess of credit and derivatives play an incongruously large role in their development and bursting. Nonetheless, it is often the absurdity of the situation that stands out: that a company renaming itself a 'dot-com' suddenly becomes significantly more valuable or that for a time in the 1980s the Imperial Palace in Tokyo could be 'worth' more than all of California[8].

Prices are a record of what we value but say little about why we value them. This surely acts as a limiting factor on the claims to rule status of any observation within the economic sphere. It also suggests that, while there is a shared economic experience (that we value things, that prices are a record of these values and so on), it is always an exercise in the particular rather than the general, and this necessarily limits our confidence in how the future will unfold economically.

A strange world emerges when one allows prices to be treated just as numbers (this includes interest rates as the price of time in monetary form). It permits us to explain price movements as the work of profit-maximising, rational agents pursuing their self-interest. In this scenario, because all actions are assumed to be rational, they are consistent and thus can be generalised into theories allowing a great degree of inference about future behaviour as it too is assumed to be consistent, since it is only ever rational. This is clearly a circular argument. It also allows price-series to be subjected to correlation analysis on the assumption that consistent, rational behaviour will ensure a reversion to the mean. If ever there were an ideal of the Enlightenment, an economic view of the world filled with rational, economic men acting consistently enough to have their behaviour formulated into rules from which the future could be induced, this has to be close to its paradigm.

Such a view makes huge claims for induction with respect to economics, based for the most part on how economic behaviour is rational in a narrow sense of being profit-maximising or utility-seeking. If this is not the case, then economics is likely claiming too much at this point. Behavioural economics has revealed that much human decision making is 'odd' or at the very least inconsistent, if not at times wilfully irrational. Likewise, non-linear functions, such as the compounding of returns over time, are key to the architecture of understanding economics and financial markets, but also immediately cause valuation difficulties for the ordinary economic 'player', especially when contrasted with more straightforward, purely arithmetic calculations.

As trading has moved from pits to screens to computer programmes, it is perhaps inevitable that fear and greed has taken a more statistical guise. It is just another chapter in the history of markets, and one that ought to be assessed not as a 'truth' of market function but in the context of market behaviour and performance in an era of fiat currency, where a massive build-up in the stock of debt has increasingly led central banks and regulators to ensure 'continuity' at all costs.

It is no surprise that trading programmes built around the observation of mean reversion have been successful in an era where government and central-bank policy has been mean-reversionary, in the sense that market bail-outs are an expression of the needs of the precautionary principle to preserve the status quo at any and all costs. The irony is that the pursuit of stability is itself a source of long-term instability, as has been well documented by Hyman Minsky[9]. The problems this creates for the future are dealt with in the final chapter, especially with respect to the function of the money system itself. Needless to say, the nature of the issue is an over-confidence in the ability to intervene in the economy, especially by governments and central banks. So, while mathematics and a reliance on numbers provides confidence in financial models' ability to predict the future and therefore to justify intervening in the economy, the more critical philosophical arguments that lie behind this mindset come not from where economics sits in relation to history but from where it sits in relation to science. This will be the subject of the next chapter.

6.

NICE IN THEORY: THE SCIENTIFIC BASIS FOR ECONOMICS

At the start of *Anna Karenina*, Tolstoy writes, 'All happy families resemble one another, but each unhappy family is unhappy in its own way.' Economies are quite the opposite, with poorly functioning ones tending to have a common list of ailments. In some ways, once one has accounted for technological changes that improve productivity, analysing a period of economic stability or benign growth involves making a list of bad things that are not happening. The economy is in good health if it is not growing unsustainably quickly, if it is not excessively indebted, if there is no rampant inflation or crippling deflation, if there are not extremes of wealth inequality, if the country's currency is not collapsing on the international markets and so on. If one were to amalgamate all the worst-case scenarios for an economy, one might end up with a doomsday situation such as the one Cormac McCarthy describes in *The Road*. If it is a legitimate exercise to define something by its opposite, then one could think of economic stability in terms of its antithesis: a Hobbesian state of nature: 'solitary, poor, nasty, brutish and short'[1].

The tenuous nature of man's existence is sadly something that is illustrated time and again, even in modernity, when society and the economy break down. Especially when communities are displaced through war or natural disaster, economic life descends rapidly into a state that might best be described as a hand-to-mouth existence. From the point of view of the individual, little can be described as more short-term in outlook than living from meal to meal. The only meaningful instance of a shorter time horizon might be the experience of soldiers in close combat, where life and death can be decided in the instant; perhaps this is the only situation that can truthfully be described as 'living in the now'[2]. Such situations are usually those where humans exist outside their habitual social and economic relations with one another.

Clearly, there is more to a having a healthy economy and society than not being in a 'state of nature', but nonetheless the contrast provided by Hobbes is helpful. 'Mutually beneficial, affluent, pleasant, civilised and long-lasting' might not be a text-book description of what constitutes a stable economy, but it is a start. While Hobbes of course runs the risk of transposing an image of life after society has broken down into the pre-social 'state of nature', nonetheless one can describe this situation as non-economic if not pre-economic. If economic activity is seen as a shared activity, it can only occur in a social context. As patterns of shared behaviour become more entrenched, in time they turn into social customs and mores that become normative. This becomes a source of continuity, leading to a sense of stability in the socio-economic sphere. There is a danger, though, in mistaking this kind of stability (the absence of extreme dislocation from war, disease, natural disasters and the like) with the idea that the natural or ideal state for an economy is one of balance, particularly if that balance is supposed to be the outcome of the ongoing processes of change, whether they be technological, demographic, political or environmental.

The idea of balance or stability as an optimal outcome or a sign that the economy is doing well is a recursive one in economics. That the classical economists of the eighteenth century felt that stability meant an economy continuing to function in a sort of circular fashion while the marginalists of the later nineteenth century thought more about the equilibrium between supply and demand in the context of economic growth does not detract from a shared mindset about an ordered and rule-obeying economic sphere. When Immanuel Kant talked about 'the starry heavens above me and the moral law within me', his search for a framework for morality was motivated by a desire to find an equivalent to the physical laws Isaac Newton had elucidated with respect to the relationship between heavenly bodies[3]. Economists from the eighteenth century onwards seem to have been engaged in a very similar exercise, consciously or otherwise.

If one looks at Adam Smith's concept of an 'invisible hand' of unseen forces balancing the often competing and contradictory desires and needs of individuals to allow economies to continue functioning over time, one can sense some intellectual debt to the Newtonian idea of a closed, rule-bound but *self-regulating* universe[4]. The subsequent marginalist approach of looking at the balancing of the forces of supply and demand, explained in a more overtly mathematical and formulaic way, also clearly borrows more directly from physics and the Newtonian framework of the universe[5].

With this in mind, the task at hand is threefold: first, to assess the grounds on which economics can claim to be scientific in the same way as the 'hard sciences' with which it aspires to be counted; second, to reassess whether the prevailing economic assumptions derived from Newtonian physics are valid, particularly with reference to the advances in our understanding of the nature of time following Einstein and, finally, to provide a synthesis between these scientific developments and our knowledge of economic history to locate the discipline of economics in its proper place, with respect to science on the one hand and the humanities on the other.

The task of assessing economics' claim to the scientific in comparison to the 'hard sciences' is best achieved by analogy, and this can be done through examining the question of testability as a measure of scientific rigour, in the sense of Karl Popper's assertion that the strength of a hypothesis can be measured by the extent to which it holds up to testing[6].

One way of exploring the 'testability' of economic theory is through an analogy involving the pharmaceutical and diet industries. The goal of both is human wellbeing, but the manner in which this goal is delivered is very different. The pharmaceutical industry is highly regulated and procedurally controlled, yet nonetheless one that continues to innovate with respect to specialised treatments for illnesses and afflictions. Its success is based around a highly organised, multi-stage system of testing and measurement, including the double-blind test whereby neither administrator nor recipient knows which treatment is the real one or which the placebo.

The diet industry on the other hand is one characterised by seemingly ever-changing fads, trends and quack remedies, but whose continued existence and hydra-headed character stems from the apparent inability of any one diet to find a complete and lasting solution to the problem of ensuring good health. Financial gain is not the question here – like the diet industry, the pharmaceutical industry is highly lucrative, and ethical questions relating to whether treating symptoms is more profitable than curing conditions are not the focus for now. The issue for the diet industry, like the discipline of economics, is one of testability, and by looking at this, we can examine the extent to which economics can claim to be scientific. It is then possible to start asking more fundamental questions about the differences between economics as a practice relating to observation and measurement on the one hand and to prediction, planning and policy on the other.

A starting point for looking at the diet industry is to realise that the word *diet* has at least two principal meanings. We all have diets in the sense that our diet is the sum of what we ingest. Diets in this sense vary, reflecting social, cultural and particularly geographic nuances, but all exist within the context of the human need to consume in order to subsist and survive. A 'diet' presented as a means of effecting a particular outcome such as weight-loss is something quite different; it is a model of consumption with a particular optimal outcome in mind. This second type of diet is something that needs testing to see if its claims are true and its benefits genuine and long-lasting.

A new diet is a type of hypothesis about consumption, and its claims need to be measured. The process of measurement is an exercise of comparison to a fixed scale unrelated to the thing to which it is compared[7]. While a new drug from a pharmaceutical company can claim to be successful if it treats the condition for which it was created without undue side-effects, the characteristics of a good diet on the other hand ultimately relate just to 'being healthy'. This seems vague by comparison, and that is because it is. To be healthy can be construed as meaning not being ill, but this is also pretty vague. Perhaps good health implies longevity, but that is a hard thing to test within the confines of the claims of a particular new diet plan (as opposed to the diets of societies experiencing longevity, such as those in Japan or in parts of the Mediterranean – but this is the other meaning of diet).

The issue at hand is the absence of a scale of measurement to allow us to move from a basic empirical observation in verbal form (healthy, unhealthy) to an objective, quantitative measure that holds true without resort to an indexical judgement ('she thought he was unhealthy'). The adjectives *healthy* and *unhealthy* are essentially relative in the same way as are *hot* and *cold*. Science has, however, moved on from hot and cold to create a series of scales (Fahrenheit, Celsius, Kelvin) allowing measurement beyond relative (verbal) judgement.

Dietary health has made many leaps forward but as yet lacks the quantitative scales to make the same claims to objectivity that measurement of temperature or mass currently can. Severe shortages of a particular vitamin have been directly linked to certain afflictions and illnesses, but the difficulty in knowing the precise quantity of any particular nutrient required has left us at best with a 'recommended daily amount'. While a system of negative rules ('do not do such-and-such' or 'everything is allowed except this') may provide a rubric to avoid extreme instability in an economy or illness in a person, it also means certainty can only exist only in dire circumstances ('you'll never be healthy if you do such-and-such regularly').

As with a chronic vitamin deficiency creating an illness that shows us why a particular vitamin is ordinarily needed, so it is often only in severe economic crises or periods of political and social dislocation that the most enduring economic truths are revealed. An example of this is how, during periods of hyper-inflation, internal measures of monetary inflation can differ radically from external measures of currency depreciation – a phenomenon noted, for example, in the inflation of Weimar Germany in 1922–3 when at various points the mark fell more quickly against the dollar and other currencies than measured inflation on the price of goods rose in the domestic economy. Naturally, this was blamed on foreign speculators, although the evidence suggests domestic capital flight was as much to blame[8]. While purchasing power parity (the idea that currency exchange rates are driven in the long term by relative price levels between countries) is an attractive idea, it is only in extreme distress that profound differences between the internal and external value of a country's money appear, particularly with respect to a loss of faith amongst international investors, and there are specific reasons for this, particularly with respect to fund flows (i.e., capital flight).

Economic autopsies of crises can yield generally observable phenomena. Gresham's law, suggesting that in a period of chronic inflation the new, bad money 'drives out' any good money, since people hoard the good stuff and try to spend the debased money as quickly as possible, is typical of this. For example, one of the reasons for the great recoinage in England in 1696 was that the new, machine-made silver coins produced by the Royal Mint were hoarded while the older, hand-struck pre-1662 coins, easily clipped and counterfeited, circulated more freely – the problem being that both the good, new coins and the old, inferior coins had the same face value[9]. In this way, the English recoinage was clearly a response to a crisis in terms of the supply of specie in the country. The observation of such extreme events does not however lend itself to making inferences about general *norms* of economic behaviour.

Learning how things can malfunction can provide an understanding of how they work, but this falls short of providing us with an understanding of how things can be optimised, let alone asserting that stability and balance are the norm. It also suggests that if causality can only be established for extreme outcomes (if you do such-and-such, the outcome is certain to be bad), it also means, by necessity, that nothing is said about the intricate and multiple strands of causality that likely overlap to create a healthy economy. This is not a question of asymmetry between good and bad economic outcomes, more that economic events, both good and bad, have non-linear outcomes that are situationally idiosyncratic through time.

Perhaps asking questions about causality here is to ask the wrong question. Lumping individual desires and needs together as Adam Smith does as a strangely serendipitous 'invisible hand' seems to be just another way of describing providence, and thus, as a term, the invisible hand expresses nothing new or incisive[10]. Another approach would be to acknowledge that there are several parallel situations that describe equally well a robust and thriving economy, each true of a particular country, period or level of development but true only of that country, period or level of development. In the same way, 'healthiness' could be defined as not being unhealthy rather than being a state of strict conformity to some ideal of health; having 'good' skin generally means not having unpleasant blemishes rather than the complete absence of imperfections that could lead to a career on the catwalk. While some habits are definitely unhealthy, we cannot infer from them a precise definition of healthiness in any distinctively positive way.

It is not coincidental that this view of health (of the body and/or the economy) is analogous to Isaiah Berlin's concept of negative liberty, which suggests one is free to do something unless it is prohibited by law[11]. A 'healthy' economy could therefore be viewed as one where there is just an absence of the traits of an unhealthy one, and there are many roads to achieving this.

A 'negative liberty' approach is not an argument for laissez-faire. Indeed, one might argue that a laissez-faire world of negligible regulation and high degrees of individual liberty (in terms of the 'private sphere') amounts to nothing more than a historical observation, but one that was later adopted variously as a policy goal and an economic model. It recalls a picture of a political and social structure from the pre-industrial world, which was less urbanised and therefore less complex, characterised by 'smaller' government and less regulation, which, in absentia, meant more individual liberty for the privileged few. That this world was periodically interrupted by war and the inevitable intrusion of government taxation (and, on occasions, currency debasement) only makes the contrast to the habitually high levels of individual liberty more apparent. It was also a world largely without the sort of growth that characterised the industrial revolution and later periods, thus lending itself to a superficial analysis of a more circular economic cycle creating a sense of long-term stability and balance interspersed with short-term fluctuations due to famine, disease and war.

The word *economics*, like the word *diet*, has a descriptive and a prescriptive use. The descriptive part relates to the past and present, while the prescriptive part naturally lends itself to a course of action to be undertaken with a view to the future. The Mediterranean diet, rich in vegetables, olive oil and so on, is often promoted due to the longevity of those who habitually consume it (i.e., those who live around the Mediterranean). Adopting such a diet in a distant country, especially one where there is less sunshine, is clearly a big imposition, even if it promises good health and longevity, largely because one needs *actively* to adhere to it for one's whole life in order to realise benefits in a similar way to those who live in the Italian countryside. This is where the two meanings of the word *diet* come into conflict and, with it, the two elements of economics – the descriptive and the prescriptive.

When we talk of laissez-faire and free-market capitalism, we do so as an ideal or optimal situation, like a diet that helps you lose weight and keep it off. Yet it may be that what we are really describing is laissez-faire, with its attractive emphasis on individual liberty, as a historical description of how things worked in countries like France or Britain (and its former colonies) before they industrialised – like the diet habitual to a certain group of people in a certain place. *Pure* free-market capitalism, particularly as a description, therefore becomes an anachronism if it is used in the context of economies and societies that have advanced beyond that stage, whether due to political, regulatory, social or technological complexity. This habit seems to be particularly apparent amongst free-marketeers in the US who overlook the key role that protectionism played in the country's development from Hamilton onwards into the nineteenth century[12]. They also tend to keep quiet about many of the less amenable elements of our ostensibly freer past, not least child labour.

The very change wrought by the industrial revolution forced political, legislative and regulatory advances that marked a break between the pre-modern and the modern era, making laissez-faire and the freedom of economic action that went with it into an ideal-type, even at the very time it was first being described and formulated as an economic model. This shows the conflict at the heart of economics as a discipline: finding the frontier between economics' descriptive and prescriptive functions. This is particularly true with respect to the issue of testability and the idea that economics can guide public policy. If the concept of the healthy economy is analogous to the healthy body in terms of it being defined by the absence of ailments, then economics as a prescriptive force appears more like the diet industry than the pharmaceutical one.

But surely this criticism is not justified given the wealth of economic data we now have that can quantify and thus substantiate economic theory and policy? In terms of negative rules (avoid such-and-such), economic history can provide a list of policy actions to be avoided due to the precedent of adverse outcomes. One example would be aggressive government deficit spending financed by central banks discounting bills serving as a situation where there is a clear threshold of spending and money printing, which ends up causing extremely high and painful inflation[13].

But this still says nothing about economic optimisation as a policy goal. In the 1990s, for example, central banks started to base monetary policy around an inflation target of 2% per annum, but one can still ask why this number is optimal or why it was chosen at all. Likewise, economic growth and a broad-based increase in wealth are generally manifesto policies put forward by the left and the right when it comes to election time in developed countries. Lifting people out of poverty is a laudable and easily justified aim when contrasted with a question about specifically how much growth or how much wealth is optimal, and even how we quantify (or qualify) what growth or wealth really amounts to. This is particularly true given the growing awareness of economic growth coming at the expense of the natural environment and therefore the long-term wellbeing of humanity in general.

The scientific question 'how much?' is one demanding an objective means of comparison in the form of a fixed scale. This allows measurement in a repeatable, verifiable and impersonal manner. This is exactly what is lacking when considering negative liberty in the context of a healthy economy or a healthy body (negative liberty meaning the absence of impediments or ailments). We know, for example, that smoking causes cancer but there is no guideline about a safe number of cigarettes to smoke a day; aside from issues of addiction, how do we really know that one cigarette a day is any worse, for example, than breathing-in the air in a polluted city every day? In this context, 'none' is a convenient answer but not necessarily the right one empirically.

Without a scale of measurement, there is no real means of testability. In terms of someone's weight, 'fat' and 'thin' are essentially pre-scientific terms, since they are relative. For health, attempts at creating a scale are as yet incomplete or have met with limited success. Something like the body-mass index (BMI) cannot account for natural variations. (Many professional athletes, like American football players or rugby players, are verging on the obese according to this scale, despite being highly trained and subject to a thorough 'fitness' regimen.)

When we think about the type of comparisons we make every day about economic relations, there is a clear tendency towards a similar type of relativism despite the hard, statistical nature of the data concerned. Terms such as *rich*, *poor*, or *prosperous* are analogous to *fat* and *thin* insofar as they are relative from the perspective of one group or from the perspective of an observer (in time or place) rather than being based on a more objective comparison to a fixed scale. We do have measures of poverty calculated in monetary terms, but these only really hold on a national basis. Poor in the developed world is not the same as poor in the developing world. The relativism of poverty and wealth really matters, not least because of the key role it plays in politics.

While the terms *rich* and *poor* have meant different things at different times depending upon one's perspective, water has and always will boil at 100 C at sea level on earth because that is how the measurement system has been calibrated. Even where we have widely used economic statistics, the nature of the numbers produced are such that there are clearly questions of qualitative equivalence and composition. The veracity of gross domestic product (GDP) as a relevant benchmark is one such example. Without going into an analysis of statistical accuracy (the black economy, work done without pay in the household and so on), it is questionable whether the monetary value of GDP's components is strictly additive in the way in which it is currently computed. Those in favour of a smaller role for government would question whether GDP generated by government spending is equivalent to that generated by the private sector. In addition, the idea of a happiness index for example reflects the sense that economic activity has a qualitative aspect as well as a purely quantitative one. It is increasingly clear that economic activity as it is currently calculated neglects long-term environmental damage that could lead to lower growth in the future, and it is arguable that this ought in some ways to be discounted back into the current annual GDP figures.

At a more fundamental level, the unit of account used for making all economic calculations is not a fixed one. A dollar may be a dollar, but the value of a dollar is not fixed. One of the jobs money is asked to do is that of numeraire or an abstract unit of value (see Chapter 4), but it has become increasingly clear that in a monetary era in which currencies float against one another, rather than being pegged to one another via a commodity such as gold, this system of measurement has been left up in the air.

The monetary unit is therefore now a variable one and this also makes it relative, since when it is not being measured against itself in terms of inflation or deflation, it can only be measured against other similar currencies whose only term of reference is their constantly fluctuating price in the international markets. The issue of relativism is so endemic that it now embedded in our everyday language. When the British government is *really* straining to show it is increasing public spending, it talks about increases 'in *real* terms' rather than in nominal or non-inflation adjusted terms. That may inhibit a riposte from Her Majesty's Opposition, but is the average British citizen really that much wiser about the meaning of the spending in question?

★　　★　　★

If measurement in economics has problems with respect to the objectivity of the scales used, it also has problems with testability. The robustness of a scientific theory can in part be measured by how successfully it holds up to the rigour of testing. Regression testing (validating an economic theory in terms of how well it holds up to historic price data) may show that economic relationships held in the past, but their claim to holding in the future are predicated on a static model of the economy that itself cannot be proven due to the same limitations. As environmentalists are wont to say, there is no Planet B, and this also means that economic theory cannot be tested in the same way as scientific theories or, for that matter, new drugs in the pharmaceutical industry. The latter has its products licenced after strenuous, three-stage assessment including double-blind testing where the specific outcome of the effect of the drug in question can be assessed *all else being equal.*

It is the absence of this 'all else being equal' that is the central problem for economics' claim to be the peer of the hard sciences. As a discipline, it is littered with hypotheses where real-world factors are suspended for the sake of theory. This list of real-world factors includes, but is not limited to: the instant and perfect dissemination of information; the absence of taxation; perfect competition; rational expectations; profit maximisation; the assumed choice of all possible investments; the absence of transaction charges; arbitrage situations not existing and so on. Regression analysis is clearly only a partial solution to this problem, and it leaves economics at its most abstract (and therefore general) and exposed to the accusation of simply being nice in theory.

The predictive aspect of economic theory thus stands in relation to the economy in the same way that weight-loss diets stand in relation to what we eat habitually. There are many ways to be healthy, many of which find themselves grounded in long-held social and cultural traditions. In the same way, many economies are stable, but stable in their own way. To say they must grow or that their wealth must increase or the distribution of wealth ought to change is to feign to impose rules upon them from the outside. What is really happening in this instance is that a discrete, possibly historical system is being taken as a model to be applied in any given situation. This is no more than economics-as-ideology where a known past situation or a hypothetical (and potentially idealised) future one is being transposed into the present. If this approach really worked, there would likely only be one, undisputed economic model. There would likewise be just one diet-book. Balanced diets, like stable economies, are ones where the successful balancing comes from habit and happenstance rather than from a homogeneity 'imposed from outside'.

*   *   *

A rational world is one that can be measured and whose events can increasingly be understood in that context. Following Isaac Newton, the attraction of looking at the economic world as one based on the interaction of opposing forces offering the possibility of balance or equilibrium is fairly obvious. Like good health, economic stability is desirable but it is not a given, nor does it necessarily endure over time, but deviations can be measured and then modelled and potentially corrected. Dividing the economy into agents whose interactions, generalised in terms of supply and demand functions, mimic the interaction of forces within a Newtonian universe, also provides a nice overall metaphor, especially if the sort of 'static equilibrium' mentioned in Newton's third law is seen as analogous to a stable economy. The conceptual approach is essentially a closed one, where the economy can be viewed from the outside and stylised as a series of interactions expressed in formulaic terms. This is both a descriptive and a critical analysis of economics, not dissimilar to the view from the quantum world of the Newtonian one as being an exercise of physics 'in a box'[14].

There is, however, a strong argument for grounding economics in physics and it starts where humans began to diverge from the rest of the animal kingdom. While humans may be unique amongst the species in that their tool use allows them to exploit the natural environment to a degree unmatched elsewhere in nature, it would be wrong to infer from this that man's use of resources is the correct starting point for economics. Such an approach would be analogous to taking a geocentric rather than a heliocentric view of the solar system. To value the world and its resources as assets in themselves (and not just resources of varying scarcity) is not just the preserve of the environmental movement. It marks a shift in the approach to economics that starts to differentiate what rules exist outside the economic sphere from those that may exist within it. In fact, it is the case that the world itself only marks the limit of physical resources available to man within the economic sphere (until the mining of asteroids begins). The real starting point is the sun and laws of physics that govern the transformation of energy, which ultimately governs all life on earth, human life included.

It would be grossly reductive to describe economic history only in terms of man's ability to harness and transform the sun's energy. Yet it is the first law of thermodynamics (that energy can neither be created nor destroyed but only transformed from one state to another), understood in the context of man's use of tools to exploit his environment, that marks out the economic sphere. The use of tools, including language, is an intricate story of the emergence of human self-awareness, awareness of the other, the aggregation of knowledge and, with it, doubt[13]. One of the consequences of the perspective gained from our self-awareness is our apparent location in time and, because of this, of our uncertainty with respect to the future. If all animals must consume to survive, then it is only humans' tool use that, both in terms of the ability to exploit the environment and the passing on of knowledge ultimately aiding survival, allows them consciously and actively to prepare for the future by saving. Saving is much more than squirrelling away. As an action that only humans undertake, deliberately saving for the future defines the sphere of economic activity. The basic economic decision is either to consume or to save.

In the early modern period, there was a productivity revolution resulting from our ability to use combustion and steam to harness the sun's energy that had been stored in the form of fossil fuel. Steam power and the factory system that developed with it meant more work could be done per capita of population. Not only did this start to transform the nature of production and consumption and put us on the long road to the standards of living we now enjoy in the developed world, but it also transformed the nature of saving.

While other animal behaviour is analogous to saving, it is habitual rather than discretionary, as it occurs without an awareness of time. Human tool-use on the other hand hugely enhances the ability to save for the future, and such saving is a phenomenon observable from the earliest, settled communities who had to save some of their harvest for replanting the following year. At this level, there was clearly a primitive awareness of the need to preserve energy (in the form of food) for the future, even if the laws of energy conservation were as yet unknown. At this level, the holding back of some agricultural produce is not so different to the squirrel and his nuts, and this is because saving does not yet allow for the possibility of being compensated for delayed gratification in the form of an interest payment of some sort. It is, however, already a conscious rather than a habitual practice. It is nonetheless in a sense a pre-economic situation, since decisions to save seed corn and the like are taken on an individual basis rather than a plural one. It is in the subsequent emergence of lending, interest and of market interactions more generally that the economy as a pluralistic entity is born.

The framework for the law of the conservation of energy, which observes that energy can neither be created nor destroyed but only transformed, provides the logical basis for a rule that underpins the whole economic sphere. This is the demand that balance sheets must balance. Given the logic of double-entry accounting, for every new credit there must be an equal and offsetting debit somewhere else. Assets must ultimately balance with debt and equity within the financial system. At the highest level, one can imagine energy emitted by the sun being absorbed by the earth through radiation and being stored by plants through photosynthesis. This creates what might be described as energy assets on earth and equivalent liabilities for the sun. If one then looks at the resources of the earth, both organic and inorganic, one can see how the story of man's economic progress is one of exploiting the natural environment to create assets, which are the earth's liabilities. The financial world's balance sheet is merely an extension of this, particularly with respect to the role debt plays in expanding the balance of assets and liabilities in the economy. While this would seem a very sterile starting point for the environmental movement, it nonetheless reflects the logical necessity of balance sheets having to balance due to the conservation of energy. It does, however, mark the boundary of the economic sphere as one of human interaction and activity and suggests that economic progress, both in terms of quantum and magnitude, must necessarily come at some expense to the natural environment.

The same balance-sheet logic applies between countries in terms of the balance of trade, as well as between governments, corporations and households within a country, all the way down to the level of the individual. The rapid acceleration of economic growth following the industrial revolution can therefore be seen as a two-stage process in terms of man's assets rising against nature's and, within the economic sphere, of how those assets were distributed between countries, institutions, companies, communities and individuals. The duality of debit and credit as accounting identities also denotes the economic sphere and, within it, the financial one, as one necessitating interaction at its most basic level and therefore is best (and in fact only) understood in terms of relations. Economics is therefore, from the outset, a relative exercise as much as one demanding quantification against an abstract benchmark.

The critical factor is that, with accounting identities, everything must net to zero. Assets must equal the sum of debt and equity. In terms of the balance of trade, a country's current and capital accounts must net to zero. Overall, global consumption and saving adds up to one (i.e., there is no other alternative), and where an individual country's investment exceeds savings, the difference, represented by its current account deficit, must be balanced by excess savings from abroad through an offsetting balance in that same country's capital account. The point is that this is a global system and one that is dynamic and relative, with government policy in one country affecting consumption, saving and investment in another as a key overall driver in terms of incentives, taxation, interest rates, trade policy and so on[16]. It is the law of the conservation of energy that is critical in this analysis rather than the Newtonian idea of a steady state. The idea of these multi-variate levels of interactions, both within individual countries and at an international level, is one predicated on change and fluctuation, where balance can by necessity only be fleeting.

If saving for the future is the defining human economic activity, then our awareness of time and especially of it having a direction of some sort (past to present to future) is supported by the second law of thermodynamics. This law states that entropy (or disorder) is a property of thermodynamic systems and that entropy can only increase, moving from a state of low entropy to high entropy. Since energy never passes to a warmer body from a colder one, the process of entropy has a clear direction, and this in turn suggests an irreversible process like the 'arrow of time'. With economic activity at its core being a matter of energy transformation and preservation, which is another way of describing a matter of choosing between consumption in the present or saving for the future, it would seem that this second law of thermodynamics provides another solid argument on which to build a time-based description of the economic sphere. Indeed, one might speculate that the effect of compound interest on saving represents on a certain level a struggle against entropy, in that the saver gets more than he or she initially possessed. The build-up of debt that tends to result from this, with its negative effects on social and economic stability, particularly in terms of income inequality, perhaps shows how dangerous and difficult this collective human undertaking is.

While one appears to be on fairly firm ground when talking about specific aspects of economics that are underpinned by the first and second laws of thermodynamics, problems arise at a more general level. The conceptual mindset of classical economics and much of what has followed it seems to have borrowed heavily from the Newtonian conception of the universe. There is nothing inherently wrong in this, only that physics has since moved on while economics has not, potentially leaving the latter in an intellectual and philosophical cul-de-sac from which it needs to be shown an exit.

Newton's first law describes how bodies stay at rest or move at a constant speed unless acted upon by an external force. As discussed above, the attraction of the Newtonian mindset for economics is obvious: economic agents play the role of Newtonian bodies; supply and demand fulfil the role of forces measured in terms of land, labour and capital and so on. Most importantly, it is a world that can effectively be measured in absolute terms and therefore fully quantified. In a Newtonian conception of the universe, if there were enough data (i.e., all of it), the exact path of the future could be mapped in terms of the interaction of bodies within it. One need only consider examples such as the Soviet planned economy or the wartime economy more generally to see that the potential goal (knowing and controlling the economy through data and calculation) is one with a distinctly Newtonian feel to it.

But physics has moved on from its Newtonian foundations. Following Einstein's special theory of relativity, measurements of time are no longer absolute (or real) but relative (and proper) depending on the perspective and positioning of the bodies being measured. Given the discussion above about how measurement in economics is already surprisingly relational (rich versus poor, cheap versus expensive and so on) and how the scales of measurement economics employs are themselves less fixed than those in physics, shifting our analysis of the economic universe to one closer to Einstein's relativistic conception of physics than to Newton's absolute one seems an appropriate step.

The conceptual leap is to abandon the 'Newtonian' world of absolutes characterised by the static modelling of the forces exerted between economic agents to an 'Einsteinian' one, where concepts of value and price are meaningful only when the position and perspective of the agent concerned is the starting point of the analysis. Despite this shift, economics remains a quantitative discipline, but one where the relationship between value and price is *proper* rather than *real*, since these are measures inherently indexical to the parties involved.

This new conception of economics is dynamic, and focuses on *the event*, not the objects involved. One can elucidate a series of general observations about human economic interaction (on an individual, collective or institutional level), but the specifics are really a matter of history and therefore of empirical fact. Economics' claim to empiricism now comes from history and not from a proto-scientific claim that prices themselves allow comparison because they are an abstract and a fixed measure of value. Time and place therefore matter on two levels: first, in the sense that economic facts are historical facts; second, that an economic analysis of value is a matter of assessing relations and perspective. Economics starts to look increasingly like a discipline whose proper assertions relate to the local and the particular, and whose claims to wider degrees of inductive knowledge are therefore self-limiting. This is particularly true when considering economics' predictive power.

There is, however, a much more significant reason to favour the Einstein idiom over the Newtonian one, and this is the transformation of the treatment of time by the former. One of the consequences of looking at economics using the natural law approach of measuring interacting forces between objects is the tendency towards explanation through static models, which compartmentalise the economy into various micro and macro relations. Yet, the great contrast between Newtonian physics and Einstein's theories of relativity is that the former has time as a fixed scale while, for Einstein, time and its passage was a matter of what was being measured and where. Classical economics (and much of what followed it) sees time as a fixed scale. The idea of the time value of money expresses this most clearly: the interest rate yield curve is an expression of the value of money through time, where time usually occupies the fixed x-axis of the graph. Adopting an approach derived from Einstein's theories of relativity rather than Newtonian mechanics effectively liberates time from the x-axis of economics. Time itself becomes a variable to be measured and valued, and it is these changes in our perspective of time that can be used to understand the various economic cycles better.

By focusing on time as a variable in valuation rather than as a fixed scale against which prices are plotted, the relationship between participants in the economic sphere also acquires a different character, and one that is inherently temporal in nature. If one were to visualise a ranking system in any given society based on the longevity of outlook of the agents (both living and institutional), one could then think about how these agents interact based upon a qualitative measure similar in principle to bond duration (the idea that a financial instrument with fixed cashflows can be assessed in terms of the weighted-average of the time at which those cashflows are received), where different agents have different time horizons in terms of how they interpret value and how they themselves are valued in relation to one another.

At the most basic level of this schema, the horizon of the individual is largely one of day-to-day subsistence. The perspective of the household is longer, often multi-generational, involving shelter, education, retirement and the like. The view of companies and institutions, less dependent on particular individuals for their survival, is necessarily longer but also qualitatively different, since their corporate survival goes beyond the specific interests of their members or employees, and whose interests can at times come into direct conflict with the personnel charged with running or maintaining them. Systems of government, the legal framework and the monetary systems attached to them tend be the most permanent features with the longest time horizon, even if within the representative system individual governments come and go with the electoral cycle. By this assessment, political risk is merely a byword for a situation where those institutions with typically long durations have an unusually short one. France during the inter-war period, when governments sometimes lasted days or merely hours, would be an example of this. Political risk in emerging market countries has a similar sense of institutional and legal fragility. Such is the biome of the economy when assessed from the point of view of the time horizons of the various economic agents that comprise it.

In modern times, government and central banks dominate the domestic economy and, by so doing, exert an influence abroad through the international impact of the level of domestic consumption, saving and investment that their policies dictate. A country's fiscal and monetary policies exert an influence over every individual, company and institution on a daily basis. The way in which taxation and other fiscal policies creates incentives and disincentives to work, spend or save also dictates who gets to spend, save and invest and the manner in which they do it. But not all of the relationships in the state are economic, and the political aspects of the relationship between the government and the people dictate the overall manner in which consumption and saving occurs.

The relationship between the executive and the electorate in representative democracies offers a clear instance of the differing time horizons of government and the governed and how they vary. Free elections gain their significance as they act as exercises in the validation or otherwise of a government's conduct where every enfranchised individual has an equal say in the governance of the country on a periodic basis. The individually least-powerful economic agent (the voter) periodically exercises a collective right to judge the most powerful. This is usually infrequent; the electoral cycle is typically four or five years. As elections approach, the importance of voters' perceptions of how well the government is performing generally rises. The influence of public opinion peaks on election day. There are, of course, occasions when a particular administration's effective time horizon can drop precipitously, but again these are usually characterised by crises resulting from exogenous events.

Many of the most difficult long-term issues facing society, especially relating to social inequality, stem from and can be exacerbated by what could be described as a duration mismatch between long-term actuarial decisions relating to demography or pensions on the one hand and the demands of electoral politics on the other. Without passing judgement on the merits or demerits of social security, entitlements and the welfare state, one can see how actuarial decisions with a very long-term horizon such as infrastructure investment, retirement provisions and social care (especially for the elderly) are not necessarily compatible with the interests of a government seeking re-election in a few years' time and therefore needing to ensure its popularity with its constituency in the short term.

This problem becomes abundantly clear when considering state retirement benefits since there can be few issues more deleterious to electoral success than raising the retirement age, even when demography and long-term fiscal probity demands a longer working life to match higher average life expectancies. It is not that welfarism is unnecessary or even a social good in itself; it is that the management of such large budgets with such long-term implications sits badly with the short-termism of electoral politics. This is despite the electoral aspect of representative government being the only way to legitimise taxation and spending and to hold to account those responsible for prior decisions relating to them.

A government elected for five years might not be the best at making an actuarial decision with a thirty-year horizon, yet representative government is the only legitimate way in which to make decisions on taxation as it alone involves consent. When viewed through the medium of duration mismatches, social conflict and its influence on politics becomes easier to analyse, and this in turn offers a route to recognising and managing these risks properly.

Looking at economic and social relations through the medium of time results in a dynamic rather than a fixed model of interaction. This does not imply a hierarchy as such – a better analogy would be a series of parallel waves, with a frequency roughly inverse to amplitude. Subsistence for the individual suggests a short frequency (daily, say) and low amplitude (the influence of one private individual rarely affects the whole of the economy on a day-to-day level). Households have a longer frequency, which might most easily be characterised by the demographic cycle of birth, death, and marriage. When aggregated in terms of demography, the household 'sector' can become the most important dynamic in the economy, shaping both the change and distribution of wealth. The influence of the baby-boomer generation would be an obvious example of this. Corporations and institutions, almost by definition, last decades if not generations, and their influence often increases with size, especially when it comes to harnessing technology or exercising political influence.

Institutional longevity is key, particularly in an era when governments tend to dominate society and the economy. The powers of taxation and money-printing do not in themselves confer on governments the ability to borrow proportionally more than a prudent household might. If this were so, then the 'buyers' strikes' such as those in the UK government bond market in the 1980s (where bond auctions drew no bids since investors felt the yield offered was too low relative to the degree of risk to the government's finances) would never have happened. 'Market access', as it is known in financial circles, is not guaranteed.

At the very least, the institutional longevity of government is greater than that of households, and this might suggest that it is safer to lend them more as there is greater certainty that they will be around to make good on loan repayments. Governments may have the right and the ability to tax, print and borrow, but hyperinflations and defaults stand as proof of the practical limits to money printing and borrowing respectively. These adverse outcomes tend to derive from the short-termism of particular administrations rather than the system of government at large, particularly if the administration's politics tend to the populist. A stable system of government, especially when characterised by a strong rule of law, is the key characteristic of economic stability. Durable institutions ensure a durable economy, all else being equal, but while durability can create stability, it cannot guarantee it.

*   *   *

When time is transposed in economics from its conventional place on the x-axis of graphs to something that is itself valued and whose value changes, the description of money as a tool with past, present and future tenses also becomes clearer. It also shows that neither money nor banking (with respect to the provision of credit) are neutral within the economy. As discussed in Chapter 4: money as a system of account essentially exists in the past tense, money as a means of exchange and payment exists in the present and, as a store of wealth, looks forward to the future. While our sense of value is anchored through experience by money as a system of account, in terms of activity, the relationship between money as a store of wealth and as a means of exchange is the most significant one, as it mirrors the economic agent's binary choice between consuming and saving. The use of credit (borrowing) can thus be seen either as dissaving (if the proceeds are used for consumption) or leveraged saving (if debt is used to invest in forward-looking enterprises such as capital projects, research or education).

In financial terms, the degree of temporal risk in an investment might therefore be understood as in some way inverse to the longevity of the institution or instrument though which the investment is undertaken. A three-month US T-Bill (or other short-dated US government bond) is the safest investment available, as the tenor is short relative to the likely longevity of the US state and its ability to repay its debt. The US dollar is also the de facto global reserve currency, and as such has an attraction inherent from this role. A three-month call option on a high-growth equity is clearly a high-risk investment, offering both a potentially large return but also a high chance of loss of premium, as one only has a short period of time to be proven correct before the option expires.

Since the monetary base and the stock of credit in the economy is constantly changing, the value of money is itself never static. Money functions best when it is able to perform simultaneously the three temporal roles of system of account, means of exchange, and store of wealth without any one role dominating to the detriment of the others. The economic cycle mirrors shifts between these functions, particularly money's roles as a means of exchange and a store of wealth. In this way, rather than just looking at inflation or deflation as a change in the purchasing power of money in terms of goods and services, one can also look at these phenomena as reflecting a shift in how we value money itself in temporal terms. This range is bound at one end in the instant by money's role as a means of exchange and extending out into the future in terms of a store of wealth. Periods of inflation reflect money's growing short-termism, as its role as a means of exchange for consumption dominates the real economy and resulting rising interest rates eventually shorten investors' time horizons in the financial economy as the implied discount rate rises. The converse is true of periods of deflation where consumption is deferred and prices fall.

In reality, though, the outer boundary of the economic horizon is marked by the lifespan of the money system itself. Rising inflation describes money's role as a means of exchange dominating. In the extreme situation of hyperinflation, money gravitates towards the instant as a means of exchange and, human behaviour being what it is, it is exchanged for anything but the money itself. When no longer acting as a store of wealth in any capacity, money increasingly ceases to act as a useful means of exchange as well – its time horizon moves to zero, too short a time span even in which to transact to create prices. The wheelbarrows of banknotes observed during Weimar Germany's hyperinflation offer a potent symbol of money's failure to function even as a means of exchange, let alone as a store of wealth.

There is a phenomenon of hyper-inflation but not one of hyper-deflation; human life assumes some degree of consumption at all times, therefore, in a monetary society, money will always continue to act as a means of exchange, however depressed the level of monetary velocity. Perhaps hyper-deflation assumes economic collapse, and one ought to be thinking here of a post-money period of barter. If hyper-inflation shows monetary-time speeding up (a foreshortening of money-holders' effective time horizon to the present), then the excesses of deflation are a slow decline in aggregate demand and therefore of consumption. Money is increasingly biased towards being a store of wealth rather than being used as a means of exchange. The unemployment and social deprivation of periods of extreme deflation are symptomatic of a collapse in consumption, and therefore of a dearth of money as a means of exchange to enable it or of credit to finance it. The collapse of credit from loan defaults during periods of extreme deflation and the risk of spiralling bank failure leading to a currency crisis mirrors the problems caused during hyperinflation, when the failure of money to perform one of its temporal roles can lead to its failure to perform all of them.

★　　★　　★

Given that consumption exists as the basic need that an economy must fulfil to be functional and that, for this reason, saving is a choice initially subordinate to consumption, one can see how the apparent direction of time implied by entropy makes these economic choices between consuming and delaying consumption via saving ones that always seem to be about time. This makes our sense of time into something flowing from a past we use as a reference point for value into a future for which we invest from the perspective of a rolling 'now'. But the appearance of time implied by this perspective is totally at odds with what we know about time from a quantum level: that it is directionless; that it does not really flow; that there is not a universal rolling 'now'. What we need to consider then is that there is in fact an economic 'now', but it is always the particular now of the economic agent being considered, even if some economic events are big enough to affect all our 'nows' simultaneously and in a similar way.

Understood from the point of view of energy transfer from consumption and the implicit rise in entropy ensuing from it, our strange perception of time starts to make sense. In addition, when one considers time and the apparent directional aspect of entropy in the context of money and particularly the use of it, one can also see how the passage of time, while it may seem linear as we look at the clock and make basic choices between consuming now or saving for later, is in fact non-linear in a money economy that involves lending for interest, and that time's passing is therefore different for debtor and creditor. All else being equal, compounding makes the lender exponentially rich and the debtor increasingly poor and the social and economic issues that tend to follow from this phenomenon provide history with its recursive character, both in terms of the various cycles (business, credit, money system and so on) and in terms of the crisis events usually marked by serious problems with the money system itself, whether inflationary or deflationary.

With price as the empirical record of value, and value reflecting our recursive economic choices between consuming and saving in the context of money, debt and interest, there is much work for the economic statistician and pattern-finder. Given the idiosyncratic nature of value itself in the context of ongoing social, cultural, political, technological and demographic change, there is also plenty of work for the economic historian. The psychological and ethical nature of our perception of value, sometimes rational and sometimes less so, then provides much for the behavioural economist to address. Left out in the wind is the fortune teller and those who meaningfully think that the past can be a perfect guide to the future. The study of economic events, particularly those of an extreme nature, may provide our clearest guide to the key functions of the economy, but they also only provide a list of actions, undertaken by governments, central banks, commercial lenders and other key entities, that ought to be avoided in the interests of preventing future instability. In that sense, at any given moment we can only really be sure of having a not-to-do list for our economic futures.

7.

IN SEARCH OF FREE TIME: SOLVING THE ECONOMIC PROBLEM

The central idea in this book is that economic decisions are fundamentally decisions about time, reflecting a basic choice between consumption in the present or delaying that consumption by saving for the future. The premise behind this is that all life on the planet depends to a varying degree on consumption through energy transfer and that, through their unique ability to harness the world's resources through technological know-how in the very long term, humans have developed to dominate their environment. This premise is not a new one. Writing at the onset of the great depression in 1930, John Maynard Keynes defined the economic problem of mankind as one relating to the ongoing struggle to provide subsistence. He felt that once technological progress and the growth of capital by compound interest had solved that problem, humans would be freed from the burden of work and could enjoy a state of 'economic bliss'. Perhaps working only three hours a day, people would be able to enjoy an 'age of leisure and abundance'[1].

It is interesting that Keynes foresaw the great saving result-ing from technological developments ultimately as being a saving of time. Some ninety years on from when he wrote this essay, sadly the Keynsian utopia, characterised in part by an end to 'love of money as a possession', has yet to manifest itself. Long working hours, poverty and income inequality still exist alongside consumerism, materialism and avarice.

Keynes was, however, prescient in his view of the likely technological progress about to be experienced in agriculture. In his book *How the World Really Works*, Vaclav Smil details, in terms of time spent, quite how revolutionary the effect of progress on the production of food has been:

> *Many people nowadays admiringly quote the performance gains of modern computing ('so much data') or tele-communications ('so much cheaper') but what about harvests? In two centuries, the human labor to produce a kilogram of American wheat has reduced from 10 minutes to less than two seconds. This is how our modern world really works.*[2]

He goes on to add that modern living – the spending of time on pursuits other than food production – would have been impossible had not 80% of the population been freed from the land by technological progress, in particular through the use of mechanised agricultural equipment and fertilisers, both of which are fully dependent on the use of fossil fuels. Yet the idea of progress resulting in *free time*, as Keynes envis-aged, has not transpired as the desired product of the growth of capital on the one hand and scientific and technological advances on the other. Smil goes on to describe the critical nature of commodities within the functioning of the global economy, and behind their usage lies the need for a source of energy to effect their extraction, production and refining. Until there is an effectively free and limitless source of energy, the economy will always be bound to problems of scarcity. With that scarcity comes decisions about consumption and saving, and this in turn continues to make economic choices ones about time.

While wind and solar offer the prospect of a limitless source of energy, the infrastructure needed to create, support and maintain renewable energy sources is high, particularly if one judges cost in terms of the 'energy return on investment' (the cost in energy terms of building and maintaining the energy infrastructure concerned). On this basis, the energy density of wind and solar is far lower than that of oil or natural gas, let alone nuclear fission. Not only do wind and solar require a huge energy input in terms of infrastructure to make them into viable energy sources, they cannot act as a store of energy in the way oil or coal can without massive investment in battery systems. These considerations exist irrespective of wind and solar being 'intermittent' sources of energy, which, unlike the more traditional sources of base-load power (fossil fuels and uranium), are weather-dependent.

Nuclear fusion is often held as a cure-all energy source, but the reality of stable fusion that yields a positive energy return has been a promise that has been just around the corner for over half a century now. Where the fusion that transforms hydrogen into helium in the sun to release massive amounts of energy relies on high levels of gravity, the lower levels of gravity on earth requires fusion to happen at considerably higher temperatures than exist in the sun, and this in turn requires massive expenditure on precision equipment, which makes the proposition of fusion as a major source of clean energy an extremely expensive one[3].

Other technologies may offer a more immediate solution to the world's energy problems, particularly with respect to emissions. The use of thorium instead of uranium in fission reactors, the use of smaller, modular (uranium) nuclear reactors with lower individual capital costs or the development of hot-rock mining technology to make geothermal energy a viable alternative to the burning of fossil fuels are all within our reach, should the capital (both monetary and political) be made available. Yet none of these are ultimately 'free' even if they are more sustainable in terms of their effect on the environment.

Until (or unless) we have access to an effectively free, clean and limitless source of energy, Keynes' aspirations for a more fulfilling human experience resulting from all that free time will have to be put on hold. A free source of energy that could guarantee our perpetual subsistence would effectively end the need to save for the future and, with it, time would no longer be a meaningful factor in the economic calculus.

If anything, the growing concern about the environmental impact of human progress and economic growth suggests that the conceptual scope of economics that has taken hold since the late nineteenth century is itself overdue a revision. While older concepts of political economy of the sort that might have been familiar to Smith or Ricardo saw the economy as a system aiming to provide continuity and social stability, the direction that economics took under the likes of Alfred Marshall was altogether narrower, where the economy was in a sense separated from society, at least in theoretical terms. The increasingly forceful assertion of the irreversible ecological damage due to man's economic progress suggests that, both philosophically and technically, economics needs once again to broaden its scope, this time concerning itself not only with society, but also with the natural environment at large.

The question of the economy's relationship with society and the environment really falls into two parts: how big is the pie, and who gets what share of it? The question of the distribution of the pie is a more traditional one relating to labour and capital's respective share of profits. Who gets what is as much a political question as it is an economic one: a question of left versus right; of socialism versus free-market capitalism, if one can still meaningfully think in such stylized terms. The question of the pie's size is a slightly different one. There has really been no economic or political movement that has aimed at the impoverishment of society, even if poverty has been the outcome of economic policy at various points in history. Economic growth resulting in improved welfare for the citizenry, whether guided by the hand of the state or left to the vagaries of the market, has always been an implicit goal for both the left and the right. In the choice between mother knows best or the market knows best, progress in terms of economic growth has always been the desired outcome.

The question of growth sustainability within an economic system is generally well understood. When economies get over-indebted, the pressure on debtors tends to undermine both consumption and eventually the ability of debts to be repaid, and this can lead to economic instability. The same is true of the social instability that tends to follow extremes of wealth inequality. With respect to the debt problem, clearly this is not just a quantitative question (how much growth, how much debt is used to drive this growth) but also a qualitative question about what the borrowing has been used to fund. If borrowing is used to fund consumption, it should generally be considered low quality. If it is used to fund investment (useful and profitable capital projects, education or research for example), it should be considered high quality. The latter is true both of public-sector and private-sector borrowing. Yet at a time when factors outside the narrow confines of the economic system are increasingly coming to the fore of public policy, these quantitative and qualitative questions are starting to broach new ground – ground previously overlooked in neo-classical economics.

While the Anthropocene era, the epoch in which human's influence on the planet has come to the fore, can be dated back as long as 15,000 years ago, in recent years its commencement has been brought forward to the middle of the twentieth century[4]. In any case, the environmental impact of economic growth now sits at the forefront of public debate. While it has so far been addressed principally as a qualitative issue – for example, in terms of clean or renewable energy as opposed to fossil-fuel energy – the much harder quantitative question has yet to be worked out. One way of posing this quantitative question is to ask whether the pursuit of economic profit from ever-increasing consumption in an open economy is any better for the environment than the sort of environmental degradation witnessed in command economies such as the former USSR. While perhaps not as visually dramatic, the long-term effect of mass consumption on global ecology can be argued to be just as devastating.

While our tendency to save as well as to consume is not in itself a reflection of an innate desire for self-improvement, it nonetheless suggests a strong natural human predilection towards accumulation, rational or otherwise. This creates a paradox: if the urge to save (and therefore to accumulate) sits at the heart of our economic rationale, and if the economy exists to serve society in effecting this, how can we square economic growth with a stable basis for society if the very growth that our economic system aims to achieve appears to come with increasingly dire ecological and environmental consequences that themselves undermine social stability and therefore the economy itself? The logic of the Anthropocene era is that human progress results in our changing the natural environment, and there are few examples where this progress has led to genuinely positive ecological outcomes. If damage limitation is the only feasible goal, what else can we do to mitigate the damage we have already done and are likely to do in the future?

If it is a question about the overall amount of consumption and its ensuing damage to the environment, then the answer to the problem of mitigating the extent of this damage can only lie within the economy itself. This logically has to be a question about the composition and drivers of consumption: how much we consume and for what purpose. These two questions are inextricably linked. If the *how much* is *too* much, then the *for what purpose* ought to be the focus, and this is very much a qualitative not a quantitative question. Who (or what) is fit to answer that question? In a planned economy, it is the state. The Soviet Union's centrally planned economic model, Gosplan, was a disaster both for society and for the environment. Wartime planned economies tend to be highly inflationary as deficit financing by governments stimulates demand far beyond the productive capacity of the economy. On the other hand, one can rely on the market to decide through the profit motive and the creative destruction of companies and sectors no longer usefully serving the economy. Yet it is becoming increasingly clear that there are many costs to the environment and to society that are not included in the profit calculus of the classic free-market, capitalist model. Capitalism has never really had to answer this question, and perhaps its narrow focus on utility and the profit motive means it cannot.

An answer may lie in the relationship between debt and consumption and how the money system links them. In 1971, President Nixon ended the Bretton Woods system, which had allowed dollars to be converted by central banks to gold at $35 per ounce. No longer anchored by a gold-backed dollar, currencies floated against one another. But the system was one in which (principally because of its use in international trade, including the pricing of oil) the US dollar continued to act as the key reserve currency asset. The new global monetary system was a fully flexible credit one, backed by good faith in government rather than gold as a monetary metal. Alongside a series of agreements to promote free trade, reduce capital controls and ease banking regulations (detailed in Chapter 2), the global stock of debt started its inexorable rise, and this process was in no small part enabled by the post-Bretton Woods monetary system.

It is not that debt is in itself bad; it has been an economic reality from the earliest forms of human society and is clearly useful when directed towards sound investment. But when one has the confluence of policies promoting free trade and the free movement of capital, social democracy and the welfare state *as well as* a fully flexible credit system of money, there is nothing to stop the process of the accumulation of debt through compound interest. The features of the classic gold standard, which moderated the growth of credit and led to economic contractions, were automatic, inbuilt and could thus be seen as *passive*. In a fiat system, policies to slow the economy, either on the fiscal front (austerity) or the monetary front (interest-rate rises), are always voluntary and therefore *active*, and the onus this puts on governments and central banks to do the right thing is immense, especially given the political and social pressures that exist in opposition if prudent policy demands that the economy must start wearing the proverbial hair shirt. In an age of far more moderate welfare support and with a monetary system based on gold, politicians and bankers in the nineteenth century were simply not confronted by this moral and economic conundrum in the same way.

The effect of debt on consumption is a multi-phased one. Chapter 2 discussed how in the UK the growth of debt has transformed residential housing from something that was essentially a good, albeit a resaleable one whose utility extends through time, into something more like an investment aimed at future profit. Rising house prices have an ongoing effect on household formation, social mobility and wealth inequality. More generally, the inexorable process of the accumulation of debt in a fiat-money system means that credit enters new parts of the economy, and it is this colonisation of the economy by debt through the process of financialisation that eventually undermines productivity and growth as the burden of debt repayment increasingly weighs on aggregate demand.

Financial and economic crises are the result. While it has been monetary, fiscal and regulatory policy choices that have sown the seeds of financialisation, the process itself is essentially a passive one, driven by the compounding effect of interest over time. Yet even these policy choices are not themselves necessarily active decisions driven by free will – social democracies, which want to promote a level of social wellbeing characterised by welfare support, pensions and public healthcare, are not compatible with a money system such as that which characterised the classic gold standard era. When gold is money, governments have, by necessity, to be small, simply because the rules demand it. Yet it is the very boom-bust credit cycle existing in the nineteenth century that paved the way for a social and political desire for greater central government involvement in the economy, first in terms of a safety net for workers, and later in the twentieth century to what we now call social democracy. It would be going too far to blame the gold standard for *causing* the shift to a fiat system of money, but the money system itself clearly plays a role in how the economy and society develop, and the vagaries of gold's effect on the economic cycle have to be considered in that historical context.

The history of money systems, particularly the shift from commodity-based money to fiat money, suggests that we end up with the money system we deserve, or that society ultimately demands. This is neither a purely active nor a passive process, but clearly there is a collective element to it, since money does the jobs we ask it to do. The character of the money system reflects the needs of the economy and society. When gold was the principal basis of money, monetary inflation was low, as money functioned well as a store of value. There were in fact extended periods of deflation, especially during the nineteenth century. Fiat money, which ultimately lacks any restraint on its own creation, functions far better as a means of exchange and payment. Because the jobs money does are not necessarily mutually compatible, there is always a calculus in terms of the benefits and drawbacks of any particular system. In the same way the ordinary language we use is not perfect in terms of its structure as a tool to convey meaning but whose imperfections allow it to evolve and change, so the flaws in money suffer the same problems while offering similar advantages. We are no closer to having a logically perfect system of money than we are to adopting a logically perfect system of language.

The existence of debt jubilees throughout history attests not only to the negative effect of over-indebtedness on society but also the periodic recognition of the need to 'reset' the system for the social good. By writing-off debts, the relation between debtor and creditor can be rebalanced, and social relations would experience a similar shift between rich and poor. In an era when governments are often the largest debtor, the tools available for them to improve their fiscal position are varied. Default is one option. Debt jubilees ought to be thought of in this category, but the political price is high, especially when currencies float against one another. Taxation is another option, as is austerity, neither of which are vote-winners. The final choice is inflation, which is itself really a tax on the value of money. While periods of high inflation can see the gap between the rich and poor shrink as capital is destroyed, the burden of inflation on the necessities of life often falls hardest on the poor as the spending power of their money declines relative to its own historic levels.

★   ★   ★

The era of the fully flexible credit system of money (fiat) has also been an age of debt, and while it is often dated as starting in 1971 with the end of the Bretton Woods system, the fiat era should be considered more as a culmination of processes originating earlier. The twentieth century can be characterised by two great trends, both of which have been 'mass' in nature. The first is the growing role of government within society and therefore the economy, whether it has been to fight wars, to promote social welfare in its various guises or simply to deal with the growing complexity of modernity as characterised by the establishment of mass democracy in the West. The second is the emergence of a mass consumer culture in which desire (wants) superseded necessity (needs) as the dominant rationale for buying things, but which itself relied on technological, demographic, cultural and social developments that allowed it to emerge and express itself when and in the specific way it did.

If one were to ask why we no longer have a gold standard, for example, the needs of big government and the pressures of consumerism provide good starting points. Both emphasise spending in the present, and this is what fiat money is good for. Gold as money clearly functioned better as a store of wealth, but this is antithetical to the ever-growing spending demands of the welfare state and a consumer economy obsessed with instant gratification and the thrill of the new (and the tendency for it to use credit to get what it wants *and now*). This is the sense in which we end up with the system of money we need or that society demands.

If one looks at debt as something with a sort of animus of its own because of its tendency to compound over time, then the *problem* with fiat money is the absence of an in-built ability to limit this debt growth over time. Using fiat money, a consumer-driven society within a social democracy will always find it hard, if not impossible, to limit the build-up of debt. One might conclude, given that the period from 1971 to the present has been the longest period in global history when money has not been tied to a physical commodity such as gold, that in fact mass consumption and social democracy *need* a fully flexible credit system of money in order to function. The question is whether history eventually shows this to have been a grand experiment of one sort or another.

If one is truly concerned about the overall level of consumption in the global economy (regardless of its quality), then one should be concerned with the growth of debt, and particularly its use to fund consumption as opposed to investment. This is the unpalatable question at the heart of the economics of climate change. If economic growth means ever-rising consumption, and if this consumption is ultimately linked by debt to the money system, is it in our money system that we will find the answer to limiting the economy's impact on the environment?

The odds of a global agreement to end the absolute level of consumption and therefore to cap global economic growth are likely nil. Not only would this mean developing economies would never be allowed to progress, it would be the ultimate vote-loser for developed economies whose governments are elected through the ballot box. More fundamentally, it goes against the human instinct to save and to accumulate for the future. In the developed world, it is possible that a much leaner economy in terms of resource consumption could be the active product of political decision-making, but this would mean a battle against the vested interests in the current system, notably corporate power.

More likely, the answer will emerge passively from the market and the money system itself, particularly as it relates to debt. If there is a reset of some sort, whether it is ultimately a deflationary one, a highly inflationary one or a combination of the two over time, any new money system emerging may have to be one where money and credit are more closely linked to the commodities that ultimately form the basis for the consumption and saving decisions that sit at the heart of the economic calculus. The progress being made within the financial industry itself with respect to the technological capabilities allowing decentralisation and tokenisation means that the money and lending of the future could bear little resemblance to that of the past. A shift from a nominalist view of money to one more commodity-based does not mean a return to the gold standard per se, even if commodities such as gold do form a part of the monetary system of the future.

Money has to do the jobs we ask it to. When it fails to do these jobs, then money itself fails and is replaced. In the developed world, the age of monarchy, patriotism and nationalism started to give way with the First World War. The lure of King and Country, empire and glory proved to be hollow, and the progression of the twentieth century in the West at least saw a shift to a type of money that allowed for new needs to be accommodated, whether this was consumer choice in the private sphere or democratically legitimised welfare support in the public sphere. In terms of money systems, the twentieth century saw the gold standard give way to a fully flexible credit system of money. Big government took the place of limited government and consumer choice dominated subsistence.

In the same way that the Great War marked the passing of the gold standard era, it remains to be seen how much further the current fiat system of money, with its propensity to accumulate destabilising amounts of debt, will be able to project itself into the twenty-first century. The challenges of unfunded liabilities (particularly relating to pensions and healthcare) in the public sector and resource scarcity and the perceived environmental cost of mass consumption in the private are increasingly seen as immanent threats. Should the promises of social democracy and consumerism, which have engendered the fiat-money era, prove to be unsustainable in the future, then much in the way the gold standard faltered after the Great War, so might the current money system stumble under the weight of its own inadequacies and failings. If that were to be the case, we should expect to see a new chapter in the history of money being opened, one in which the money of the future is a better fit for the job in hand.

BIBLIOGRAPHY

INTRODUCTION. THE MARSHMALLOW TEST REDUX

1. Mischel, Walter, *The Marshmallow Test – Understanding Self-control and How to Master It*, (Little, Brown, Spark/London, 2019) pp21–4.

2. Watts, T.W., Duncan, G.J., and Quan, H., 'Revisiting the Marshmallow Test: A Conceptual Replication Investigating Links Between Early Delay of Gratification and Later Outcomes', *Psychological Science*, vol. 28, no. 7.

3. *Can Kids Wait? Today's Youngsters May Be Able to Delay Gratification Longer Than Those of the 1960s*, American Psychology Association, (25 June, 2018).

4. Keynes, J. M., *Economic Possibilities for Our Grandchildren*, (1930), *Collected Works*, Vol. IX.

5. Rovelli, Carlo, *The Order of Time*, (Penguin/London, 2019), p15, p30, p40.

CHAPTER I. TIMELY MEDITATIONS

1. Pierce, Andrew 'The Queen Asks Why No One Saw the Credit Crunch Coming', *Daily Telegraph*, (5 Nov. 2008).

2. Bowden, Mark, *The Last Stone*, (Grove Press/UK, 2019), pp17–8.

3. Scruton, Roger, *Modern Culture*, (Bloomsbury/London, 2014), p15.

4. Keynes, J.M., *A Tract on Monetary Reform*, (1923).

5. Meyer, Robinson 'The Cataclysmic Break That (Maybe) Occurred in 1950', *The Atlantic Magazine*, (16 April 2019).

6. Koselleck, Reinhart, *Futures Past*, (Columbia University Press, 2004), pp13–5.

7. Ro, Sam, 'DRAGHI: Whatever It Takes', *Business Insider*, (26 July 2012).

8. Jähner, Harald *Aftermath: Life in the Fallout of the Third Reich 1945–1955*, (WH Allen, 2021), pp161–3.

9. Pepys, Samuel, 'Tuesday 4th September 1666', *The Diaries of Samuel Pepys: A Selection*, (Penguin, 2003).

10. Neustadt, Richard E., & May, Ernest R., *Thinking in Time: The Uses of History for Decision Makers*, (The Free Press / Collier Macmillan, 1988), p156.

CHAPTER 2. AN ENGLISHMAN'S HOUSE IS HIS LADDER

1. 'Remembering the Beast from the East', *Weather Watchers*, (bbc.co.uk, 16 Feb. 2019).

2. Gordon, Robert J., *The Rise and Fall of American Growth*, (Princeton University Press, 2017), pp351-2.

3. Holmans, A.E. 'Housing Policy in Britain', *English Housing Survey Headline Report* (Office of National Statistics Data, Croom Helm, 1986, 202–1).

4. Grossmith, George & Grossmith, Weedon, *The Diary of a Nobody*, (1892).

5. Smith, David, *The Rise and Fall of Monetarism*, (Penguin, 1987), p39.

6. Tversky, A. & Kahneman, D., 'Loss Aversion in Riskless Choice: A Reference Dependent Model', *Quarterly Journal of Economics* vol. 106, no. 4

7. Connolly, Bernard, *The Rotten Heart of Europe*, (Faber & Faber, 2012), pp71–2.

8. 'There Is More to House Prices Than Constrained Supply', *The Economist*, (24 Nov. 2018).

9. 'Why Japanese Houses Have Such Limited Lifespans', *The Economist*, (17 Mar. 2018).

10. Wittgenstein, Ludwig, *The Blue Book*, (Blackwell, 2008), p18.

CHAPTER 3. FOR WHAT IT'S WORTH: THE NATURE OF VALUE

1. Kahneman, Daniel, *Thinking Fast and Slow*, (Allen Lane, 2011), pp32–7.

2. Dummett, Michael, *Origins of Analytic Philosophy*, (Harvard University Press, 1994), p4.

3. Wittgenstein, Ludwig, *Philosophical Investigations*, (Wiley-Blackwell, 2009), Part 1, Section 43.

4. Hutton, Ronald, *Pagan Britain*, (Yale University Press, 2015), p257.

5. Carlyle, Thomas *Chartism*, (1840), Chapter 6.

6. Smith, Adam, *An Inquiry into the Nature and Causes of the Wealth of Nations*, (1776), Book I, Chapter 1, pp3–4.

7. Popper, Karl, *The Open Society and its Enemies, Volume 1: The Spell of Plato*, (Routledge, 2007), pp190–1, pp199–202.

8. Thomson, William the Lord Kelvin, 'Electrical Units of Measurement', (delivered May 1883), *Popular Lectures and Addresses* Vol. 1, (1889).

9. Menninger, Karl, 'Our Own Numerals', *Number Words and Number Symbols*, (Dover, 1992), p391.

10. Lewis, David, '"Might" Counterfactuals and Outer Modalities', *Counterfactuals*, (Blackwell/Oxford, 2005).

11. Horwich, Paul, *Truth*, (OUP, 1998), pp8–9.

12. Boyce, Robert, *The Great Interwar Crisis and The Collapse of Globalization*, (Palgrave Macmillan, 2009), pp11–13.

13. Zweig, Jason, 'Let's Be Honest About Gold: It's a Pet Rock', *Wall Street Journal*, (17 July 2015).

14. Ricardo, David, *Principles of Political Economy and Taxation*, (1817), Chapter 7.

15. Marx, Karl *Capital*, (1867), Vol. 1, Chapter 1.

16. Malthus, Thomas, *Essay on the Principle of Population*, (1798).

CHAPTER 4. THE MONEY VALUE OF TIME

1. Wray, L. Randall, *Modern Money Theory*, (Palgrave Macmillan, 2015), pp41–44.

2. Davies, Glyn, *History of Money from Ancient Times to the Present Day*, (University of Wales, 2002), pp289–90.

3. Graeber, David, *Debt: the First 5000 Years*, (Melville House, 2014), pp58–9.

4. Piketty, Thomas, *Capital in the Twenty-First Century*, (Belknap Press of Harvard University Press, 2014), pp104–5.

5. *Special Drawing Rights*, www.imf.org, (24 Mar. 2020).

6. Triffin, Robert, *Gold and the Dollar Crisis*, (Yale University Press, 1966), Part I, p68.

7. Hudson, Michael, *And Forgive Them Their Debts: Lending, Foreclosure and Redemption*, (ISLET-Verlag Dresden, 2018), p17, pp21–2.

8. Ibid., pp24–5.

9. Piketty, Thomas, *Capital in the Twenty-First Century*, (Belknap Press of Harvard University Press, 2014), p271.

10. Ibid., p271.

11. Werner, Richard, *Princes of the Yen*, (Quantum Publishing, 2018), pp132–3.

12. Bernholz, Peter, *Monetary Regimes and Inflation*, (Edward Elgar Publishing, 2003), pp18–19.

13. Knapp, Georg Friedrich, *The State Theory of Money*, (Macmillan, 1924), p15.

14. Wray, L. Randall, *Modern Money Theory*, (Palgrave Macmillan, 2015), p199.

15. Ibid., p249.

16. Jähner, Harald, *Aftermath: Life in the Fallout of the Third Reich 1945–1955*, (WH Allen, 2021), p191.

17. Chingono, Nyasha 'Dirty Dollars: How Tattered US Notes Became the Latest Street Hustle in Zimbabwe', *The Guardian*, (17 Nov. 2021).

CHAPTER 5. SAFETY IN NUMBERS: SAVING, INVESTING AND THE URGE TO COUNT

1. Menninger, Karl, 'Historical Gradations', *Number Words and Number Symbols*, (Dover, 1992), p56.

2. Aquinas, Thomas, *Summa Theologica*, 2–2.

3. Chancellor, Edward, *Devil Take the Hindmost*, (Plume Publishing, 2000), pp14–7.

4. Menninger, Karl 'The Westward Migration of the Indian Numerals', *Number Words and Number Symbols*, (Dover, 1992), p400.

5. Boxer, Alexander, *A Scheme of Heaven*, (Profile Books, 2020), pp189–92.

6. Berlin, Isaiah, *Three Critics of the Enlightenment*, (Pimlico, 2013), pp51–5, pp208–9.

7. Koselleck, Reinhart, *Futures Past: On the Semantics of Historical Time,* (Columbia University Press, 2004), p13-5.

8. Parkes, Douglas, 'Japan in the 1980s: When Tokyo's Imperial Palace Was Worth More than Califormia and Golf Club Membership Cost US$3 Million', *South China Morning Post,* (1 Jul. 2020).

9. Minsky, Hyman P., *The Financial Instability Hypothesis* (Working Paper No. 74), (Levy Economics Institute, 1992).

CHAPTER 6. NICE IN THEORY: THE SCIENTIFIC BASIS FOR ECONOMICS

1. Thomas Hobbes, *Leviathan,* (Oxford World Classics, 1998), Part I, Chapter 13, 9, p84.

2. Adam Curtis, *The Living Dead,* BBC documentary (1995), Part 1 'On the Desperate Edge of Now'.

3. Kant, Immanuel, *Critique of Practical Reason,* (Cambridge University Press, 2015), p129.

4. Smith, Adam, *An Inquiry into the Nature and Causes of the Wealth of Nations,* (1776), Book IV, Chapter 4.

5. Roncaglia, Alessandro, *The Age of Fragmentation: A History of Contemporary Economic Thought,* (Cambridge University Press, 2019), p24.

6. Popper, Karl, *Conjectures and Refutations,* (Routledge/London, 2008), pp47–8.

7. Carnap, Rudolf, *An Introduction to the Philosophy of Science,* (Dover, 1995), pp63–5.

8. Ringer, Fritz K. (ed.), *The German Inflation of 1923,* (OUP, 1969), Part II, pp43–4. Fergusson, Adam, *When Money Dies,* (Old Street Publishing, 2010), p133, pp145–6.

9. Levenson, Thomas, *Newton and the Counterfeiter,* (Faber & Faber, 2009), p111.

10. Graeber, David, *Debt – the First 5000 Years*, (Melville House, 2014), p44.

11. Berlin, Isaiah 'Two Concepts of Liberty', *The Proper Study of Mankind, An Anthology*, (Farrar, Straus and Giroux, 2000), pp194–5.

12. Hudson, Michael, *America's Protectionist Takeoff 1815–1914*, (Garland Publishing, 1975), pp29–30.

13. Bernholz, Peter, *Monetary Regimes and Inflation*, (Edward Elgar Publishing, 2003), pp11–2.

14. Smolin, Lee, *Time Reborn*, (Penguin, 2014), p44.

15. Tallis, Raymond, *The Knowing Animal*, (Edinburgh University Press, 2005), pp197–8.

16. Pettis, Michael, *The Great Rebalancing*, (Princeton University Press, 2013), p19.

17. Hudson, Michael, *And Forgive Them Their Debts: Lending, Foreclosure and Redemption*, (ISLET-Verlag Dresden, 2018), p69.

CHAPTER 7. IN SEARCH OF FREE TIME: SOLVING THE ECONOMIC PROBLEM

1. Keynes, J.M., *Economic Possibilities for Our Grandchildren* (1930), *Collected Works* Vol. IX.

2. Smil, Vaclav, *How the World Really Works: A Scientist's Guide to Our Past, Present and Future*, (Penguin Viking, 2022), p51.

3. Turrell, Arthur, *The Star Builders: Nuclear Fusion & the Race to Power the Planet*, (Weidenfeld & Nicolson, 2021), pp215–6.

4. Meyer, Robinson, 'The Cataclysmic Break That (Maybe) Occurred in 1950', *The Atlantic Magazine*, (16 Apr. 2019).

INDEX

accounting 125–6, 171
  accrual accounting 172
  marking-to-market 109
  money as system of account 8,
    108, 120, 121, 124, 125–6, 127,
    130, 171, 236, 237
  relational process 125
accumulation 168
  propensity to accumulate 169,
    247, 256
  see also saving
aggregate demand 51, 174, 238, 250
agricultural communities
  early 128–9, 224
  seed saving 128–9, 141, 224
amortising debt 59
analytical philosophy 7
animal behaviour 3, 4, 224
Anthropocene Era 19, 246, 247
antiques 175
apocalypse *see* end-of-days
  scenarios
Aquinas, St Thomas 174
artificial intelligence (AI) 113
asset-price bubbles 49
asset-price inflation 153–4
  QE-induced 154
astrology 198

austerity 159, 249, 252
  political choice 159
automation 112, 113

baby-boomer generation 15, 44,
  53, 234
bailouts 6, 23, 26, 41, 48, 161
balance of trade 225, 226
balance-sheet logic 225
balance-sheet repair 21
Bank of England 41, 43
  post-GFC monetary policy 41
bankruptcy 81–2, 189
banks, banking
  bailouts 6, 23, 26, 41, 48, 161
  bank failure 6, 22, 26, 125, 238
  bank runs 22
  banking cycle 21
  capital leveraging 149, 156, 157
  credit 135, 140, 155, 156, 163
  liberalisation of 44, 45
  reserves 152, 153, 156, 163
  see also central banks;
    commercial banks
barter economy 24, 116, 117, 120,
  139, 238
Basel agreements 157
bear market 87

INDEX